Little Things in a Big Sky

A Collection of Short Stories

by Matt Troy

LITTLE THINGS IN A BIG SKY
A Collection of Short Stories
Copyright Matt Troy, 2013

ISBN 978-0-9912692-0-4

Cover design by James Sudeikis
Editing by Rob Bignell, Inventing Reality Editing Service

Manufactured in the United States of America
First printing December 2013

DEDICATION

For King Arthur, George Washington and Big Bird.

I bet that trifecta has never been mentioned in the same book dedication!

Table of Contents

I'll Trust You with My Life

During the last 18 hours, I've heard the life stories of two individuals whom I had never met prior to our conversations.

One of them was that of a 27-year-old medical student from Indianapolis, and the other a 53-year-old volunteer fire chief from a small town in east Tennessee. Their stories were vastly different, and yet I had nearly the same thought after hearing them: "Wow, I can't believe this person I've never met before was just willing to share their life story with me."

The med student and I met on the basketball court. I was out doing my evening shooting at the local high school, and he rolled up initially looking for a pump to inflate his newly purchased basketball. He seemed friendly enough, but he stayed in his car a few minutes and I went over to the court and began to shoot around. He strolled up a few minutes later and began to shoot at the goal on the opposite side of the court. About two minutes later I came over to the bench where I always leave my water bottle, which was closer to his end of the court. At that time we struck up a conversation that started with small talk about how it had been too long since he'd been out to the court. When the conversation ended two hours later, we were standing underneath his basket in the complete darkness of the night.

By then I knew he was a medical student from Indianapolis. I knew about his motivations for being in medicine, his father's support and calming influence in his life, his path to wind up in medical school, the names and back stories of some of his closest friends, the uncertainty of how he might pay off his loans, his views on whether to pay NCAA athletes, his tremendous knowledge of the TV show "The Wire," his viewpoints on the current administration at his medical school, historical race relations in Nashville, and the fact that we lived in the same apart-

apartment complex.

All the while this was going on, we were hoisting jump shots, and tracking down bounding basketballs before they left the court area.

This morning, I woke up and drove to Knoxville, Tennessee, to interview a man for a research project I'm doing for one of our clients. We agreed to meet at a Cracker Barrel off of I-40 at 11 a.m. Unfortunately I forgot that Knoxville is in the Eastern Time Zone, and thus I would lose an hour coming from Nashville. Thankfully the man was understanding, and we met at 11:30. I had planned to be a half hour early, but with the time change, that turned into a half hour late!

For the next four hours, our poor Cracker Barrel waitress had to continue to check on us as we talked about tools, selling strategies, and the state of the auto collision equipment industry (It's a fledgling industry in case you were curious).

Intertwined with these insights, I also learned about this man's life. The house he bought in 1988 at the corner of a used car lot in a little town 45 minutes north of Knoxville. The great blizzard of '93, the dissolution of his marriage in '97, going to work for Auto Zone part time, working for a man named Conrad in '03 (Conrad apparently still owes him $14,000), meeting his current girlfriend in '06, having the most prosperous year of his life in '07, the drama that forced his exit as volunteer fire chief in his hometown, starting his own business three years ago and finally, his affinity for surgically implanted cosmetic augmentations to the female form...

I sheepishly ordered chicken tenders at a business lunch (as usual), he had meatloaf, our server emptied about three gallons of water into our glasses, and we just talked. And talked. And talked. He was honored I was interviewing him for my project and more than happy to share his experiences with me. He was honest, he was candid, and he was genuine.

I was grateful for the information he was able to share, as it helped me get some critical data for my project, but more than that, I was floored by his generosity. I had called him up out of the blue two days before and asked him to meet a complete stranger for lunch to talk about a field research project regarding an obscure tool. He cleared his schedule, drove 45 minutes to meet me, and gave me four hours of his time. In the life of a sales guy, four hours may as well be a couple of eternities...

As I drove home from Knoxville, I had plenty of time to reflect on what had happened over the last eighteen hours. The biggest thing that hit me was trust. I had spent six hours hearing the most intimate details of these two men's lives. It hadn't been the goal of these encounters, but it had been the result. Complete strangers trusting me with the detailed information that made them who they are. Hardship, vulnerability and triumph. Details I didn't ask of them, but details they had shared in the name of human connection. Details that would help us relate on a deeper level. Details to help us better understand and enjoy our time together.

As I left each encounter, I exchanged contact information with both guys. We planned to stay in touch, and I sincerely hope that we do. I think I have a better chance of doing so with the medical student, considering he's my age, lives in my apartment complex, and we share common interests. But I hope to stay in touch with the sales guy as well.

Either way, the openness that we shared, the vulnerability it took to share our stories, and the deep sense of connection that I felt from it was one of the best feelings I've ever felt in my entire life. And, the best part of it was that these were complete strangers with whom I had no previous relationship at all. Their candor, their trust, and their openness is a driving force behind this book.

These are the stories of my life. They are stories of the everyday occurrences, and the joys that result from them. These are little things, but they are addends that when summed up make life worth living.

As you read, I hope that you'll laugh, that you'll cry and most of all that you will then go out and share your stories. Connect with the people and the world around you. Look more closely at the small stuff and appreciate it for what it is. You'll be glad you did!

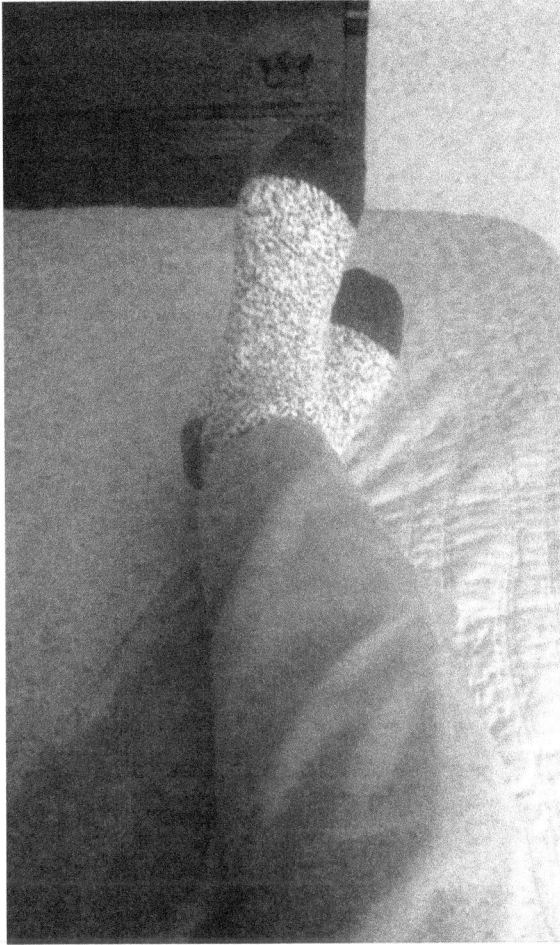

How Great are Wool Socks?

I t would be fun to lay out a store based on how the items in each section made you feel. It would be a logistical nightmare, of course, but that's not really the point. This would be a store with everything you could ever need, and nothing would be categorized like a regular store.

In the Relief section, you might find things like cold medicine that could be found in a typical pharmacy. But also in this section would be things like car batteries, ink cartridges, obscurely shaped light bulbs, and apple pie spice.

These are all things that you go to the store in need of, when you need them. And because of this fact, there is rarely joy in purchasing these items. You buy them when you need them, and after doing so, you feel relieved that you're able to check them off of your list.

Somewhere next to the relief section is the Pick Me Up section. Items like coffee, cheesy romantic comedy movies, perfume, aesthetic car accessories, and of course women's shoes would be in this section. This is the section you visit on Friday after a long week at work, and just indulge yourself a little bit. Pick up a nice little Rom-Com, maybe a box of Junior Mints, buy some functionally pointless but cool decal for your truck, and then go park yourself on the couch and relax.

Your sections might differ from mine…

Perfume might actually fall into my Would Only Buy for Others, and Even Then Maybe Never section. There might be a lot of items in this section for me…

And certain movies might be all over the store.

"Sweet Home Alabama" would be in my Pick Me Up section— along with most anything Reese Witherspoon does—while "Rush Hour 2" might be in the Don't Buy This, It Will Be On TBS Next Week, But Thanks for Reminding Me I Like It section.

Deodorant and bananas, same section. Everyday staples.

Contact solution? The Come to This Section Every Six Months for Peace of Mind section. You know, you buy things like sun screen, large trash bags, furnace filters, powdered sugar. These items aren't quite like relief items in the sense that you're not buying them out of obligation or to alleviate a current stressor, but these are just things you don't buy all that often. You knowingly stock up on them, and then don't think about them for about six months.

I haven't hit every section in my store, but I do know the last section. Without a doubt, wool socks would have their own section in my dream store.

Wool socks represent all that fine and good on this little earth we live on.

You can wear wool socks on a hiking adventure, working in the snow, or simply for comfort on a crisp fall day. For fun, for function, or just because.

They are well-made and built to last.

Wool socks go with everything, even if they don't match.

Their speckled pattern in unintentionally intricate, and at the same time, non-descript.

Wool socks always seem to be the right size, even if they are too big. If they're too small, they have just enough give to fit snugly. They cover your toes just right, without scrunching your pinky toe or impeding the natural range of motion you'd have otherwise.

Wool socks are warm. On a cool fall morning when your toes are cold, heat almost radiates out of them as soon as you put them on. After you've had them on a while, you can almost feel the warmth making its way up the rest of your leg and into your core.

Wool socks are nostalgic. You put them on and you think of snowball fights as a kid, or drinking hot cocoa after spending an hour and a half clearing the driveway of snow. You think of apple orchards or a college football tailgate.

Wool socks are a living family heirloom. A mom, a dad, a teen-ager, or an infant can't all agree on much, but it's hard to argue with a pair of wool socks. They aren't cool, but they aren't so uncool they can't be worn. They aren't sexy, but they aren't so masculine a woman won't wear them. They aren't outdated, out of style, or out of touch. As they rarely wear out, and it's not uncommon to hold on to them for years a time. Wool socks are perfect.

The Cactus Ball

This cactus ball is so ridiculous, yet it's one of my favorite possessions.

Here's what makes it so awesome: First of all, my grandma gave it to me, and anything my grandma gave to me is awesome. Not because the item itself is actually so awesome, but because imagining the thought process behind what went into buying it is drop dead hilarious.

Grandma's thought process: "Ohhh, well look at that. Isn't that cute. You know who likes balls? Matt does. You know, I think I'll get this for him. I bet he'll love it. (Picks up ball, holds in hand, looks a little more closely, checks price tag, thinks, "Oh, that's not bad" and goes to counter.)

I can't tell you how many different types of balls my grandma gave me through the years. Golf balls that are painted like soccer balls, footballs, and baseballs. Baseballs with presidents' faces on them. Baseballs with lizards on them. A random ball that was the size of a baseball but had the dimples of a golf ball, and was labeled at a flea market as a softball. Go figure. Gram got it in her head that I liked balls, and by golly, she was going to get me every possible kind she could find. But this one took the cake.

The second part of its awesomeness is the fact that it even exists at all...What is a cactus ball anyway? And why does it even exist? This one is made of very thin plastic, and is probably the weight of a ball you might find in the ball pit at an old Discovery Zone, or Leaps and Bounds (Bazinga!). It's textured on the side to make each of the surfaces appear as though it takes the shape of a cactus...albeit a non-existent spherical one...And it has approximately 1,134 (I tried to count) little hair-like spikes that stick out of little pods of seven that have been hot glued to the green cactus surface. Unlike a real cactus, on which these spikes are actually called glochids (just looked that up), these protrusions are not sharp. They actually feel as though they are slightly thicker than the bristles on a coarse horse-haired brush. Because if you were going to make a cactus ball, of course you'd want to make the faux glochids feel this way...

Which leads me to my next thought: Who thought of this idea? Honestly. For many years, there actually was a tag on this ball that had a company name on it. I'd give almost anything to remember who the company was that made this thing.

At what point was a cactus ball a good idea? Has anyone ever seen a cactus and thought, you know what, I wish that thing was spherical so we could play catch with it? Are there any other plants that companies make toys out of that aren't traditionally round to play catch with? Were they just envious of the pine cone? Are there more things to come in this line of thinking? Soon are there going to be plastic balls in the shape of milkweed plants? You know, nectar/liquid bearing plant balls are all the rage right now...

What do other people think of the cactus ball? Do kids like it? Are they like, "Dad, can we throw around the cactus ball after dinner?" Do moms secretly despise the cactus ball because it teaches kids that cacti are fuzzy, and something you can just throw around like it's a hot potato or a dog toy? This is just so misleading...

How many cactus balls did the Cactus Ball Selling Company forecast to sell this year? "You know boss, I think it's going to be a big year for my cactus balls!" said no one, ever.

To the lady in the museum gift shop, what trend exactly were you thinking was going to hit when you gave the okay to order in that last batch of cactus balls? And to the lady who bought them wholesale to sell them at a flea market so that my grandma could buy this one for me, THANK YOU.

The cactus ball is so awesome I even played with it once. There was one time not too long ago that I remember actually taking the tag off and throwing this thing around for a while. I'm really not sure why, or with whom, but something must have come over us to just think, you know what, let's play catch with the cactus ball...

But now, I don't play with it any more. I let it sit in its spot, in its own decorative soap dish in my guest bathroom. This is obviously the spot that any respectable adult keeps their cactus ball...

So, if you ever come visit, and spontaneously want to start playing catch, have I got a treat for you!

Sun through the Blinds

I t's nice to wake up early and see the sun coming up. In my room, there are two windows to the left of my bed as I lay in it. There are white wooden blinds that cover the windows. They are the slatted kind that are held together on each side by string. For the most part, they do an excellent job of keeping unwanted light out of my room. I love the sun, but I like to keep it dark in my house so that it stays cooler in the summer. Living on the first floor of my apartment complex is nice, because the heat rises, and my rooms are—in a way—insulated, and stay very comfortable, even without the use of air conditioning.

I've never really given much thought to blinds before. At times during my childhood, they played a very prevalent role in my life, but I don't think I yet appreciated it.

When I was very young, my mom would come into my room each morning and make quite the ordeal of opening my blinds. In my childhood room, the blinds were a creamish-yellow, and with the morning sun shining on them, they almost seemed to radiate, with the two shades of yellow coming together. Those blinds were the kind that operated on a twisting rod that screwed into the top of the blinds and hung down to comfortable level to crank the blinds open with a thumb and forefinger.

As she cranked the blinds open each morning, Mom would burst into song. Always the same song, and always with a boisterous energy that defied the other 98% of her personality:

Let the Sun Shine In! And face it with a grin.
Smilers never lose. And frowners never win!
So let the sun Shine in, and face it with a grin!
OPEN up your heART AND LET THE SUN. SHINE. IN!!!!!

The punctuation is important to note, because as she cranked the blinds, certain parts of the song were emphasized as she reached certain points in the blind-opening process. If you look at the printed lyrics of this song, "Sun Shine" as I have it, is actually written as one word, "sunshine," but that's not how mom ever emphasized it. You see, the entire point of this exercise was to let the sun shine into my room, and thus the verb, shine, was always the important word in the phrase.

I had two windows in that boyhood room, and two separate sets of blinds. About halfway through the lyrics, mom would make her way over to the second twisting rod, and begin to open the second set of blinds. The words building in a crescendo, until during the final line she was almost bellowing with delight. Starting with the word heart in the last line, her voice raised to its loudest level, and each word was enunciated singularly. By the end, my room was fully illuminated with the yellow light that would become—and to this day still is—my favorite color. The only thing that could match the smile on mom's face, was the smile on mine. I cannot imagine a better way to wake up each day, and it's funny, in my memory, it never rained. Every morning of my childhood was sunny. Obviously, there were plenty of days where it must have been raining or overcast, but I don't remember any of them.

I would have to think that a lot of my disposition as a person was shaped by this song. Each day to wake up to such a positive message. Smile. Enjoy the sun. Open up your heart. In a way that I could not possibly understand at the time, my mom was helping shape me into who I am today.

A lot has changed throughout the course of my life. My boyhood room is an office. The yellow blinds are gone, and I doubt too many songs come projecting out from between those walls these days.

My current room is far away, with different colored blinds that never open or close.

But, every morning as I lay in bed, readying to start my day, I look over to those blinds. At the end of each slat, there is slight gap that lets the sun in. Directly outside my windows stand a couple of large leafy trees. A mixture of the morning breeze, and the morning sun rustle the leaves so that the shadow of their silhouettes dance against the outside of my blinds. From my bed, this is a sight to behold.

Seeing the outlines of the leaves, and the glimmer of the sun through the slats is all the trigger I need, and mom's words come rushing back.

Let the sun Shine in, and face it with a grin!

I smile, get out of bed, and off I go.

Many days, around the same time, I get a text message from my mom that simply says: :-)

I'm smiling too, Mom. I'm smiling, too.

The Power of the Ocean

T he ocean is an amazing organism. I've forgotten nearly all of the facts I learned about just how amazing it is, but that's beside the point.

I once took a class in college that was simply called, "Oceans." I needed a science credit, and "Oceans" seemed about as non-complex a science class as my little brain could handle. I think I got a B- in that class. I struggled to stay awake in lecture every day, and I can't for the life of me remember my professor's name, what he or she looked like, or even the name of the lecture hall where we had class (I can picture the lecture hall and I think it might have been David Kinley Hall, but I'm not positive), and yet somehow "Oceans" turned out to be one of my favorite classes of college. I'm not sure what that says about me, the University of

Illinois, or my memory, but I digress. I do know oceans are big, are the site of a lot of complex seismic activity, and a lot of things live in the ocean. I told you, I got a B-...

Anyway, as usual, the reason that I love oceans is the role they play in the larger metaphor that is my life.

I love the ocean because of its endless possibilities. As you watch from the beach, the ocean fades out into and beyond the horizon line. In your mind's eye, what lies beyond that horizon line is up to you. Perhaps it's simply all the water that's out there, because after all, there's plenty of that. Perhaps it's the millions of organisms living just below the surface that stimulate more activity than the human mind can even imagine. And perhaps it's the endless possibilities of our own lives, and a constant reminder of how we should live them.

The ocean is beautiful. It's peaceful. It's picturesque.

The ocean is consistent. Not every day is the same, yet every day the tides rise and fall, on their own schedule. In accordance with a higher power (Author's Note: I can't remember exactly how the moon affects the tides, but I know it does. B-, I'm sorry.)

The ocean is complex. There are a million things going on at any one time under the surface. The earth is literally trying to tear itself apart at the core of the ocean, and yet at the surface, it's calm and breathtaking.

The ocean is a signal. Each day in the east, the sun rises. Sunlight beams down through the clouds, and with it, the first signs of a new day. The waters are calm, with the waves only starting to kick up. Creatures spring to life, rejuvenated and ready to live their days to the fullest. Life may rage on in the middle, but at the end of the day, the sun sets to the west.

The waning light filling the sky, signaling to all that the day is coming to an end. The waves again calm, lapping against the shore in a melodic tone that readies us to sleep. To rest. To recharge. To reflect on the day that has gone, and offer us the promise that with the tide, so too comes another day. Another day to enjoy the splendor of all it has to offer. And on, so it goes.

The ocean fills postcards. The photos, and the memories that fill our lives with joy. The clouds. The waves. The sun. The sand.

The smiling faces of visitors, friends and family members.

For me, the ocean is a reminder of those postcards. Not so much the memories in the past tense, but for the blessings of the present tense. Beneath the surface of the ocean, there will always be turmoil. There will always be seismic change, and uncertainty. But every day the ocean in beautiful. Somewhere, the sun peeks through the clouds. Somewhere the waves crash therapeutically, and somewhere in the world, at almost any given time, the sun is rising on a new day, with new blessings, and photo opportunities for the postcards that make up our lives.

Stop and Think

We were doing a video intro for a new innovative line of machinery this week at work, and of course, we showed images that included Thomas Edison, and the Wright Brothers. They represent three of America's most noteworthy inventors, and undoubtedly some of the most important. But then I got to thinking on my way to the office in Geneva...What about all the other inventions out there? And so I started to look around...

A stop sign. A manhole cover, a riding lawnmower, with a guy wearing noise-cancelling headphones.

And my mind just started spinning thinking about all of the inventions that went into those few items. Creating the alloy for the metal in the sign. The template to cut it out. The machine to execute the cut. The automatic paint machine, and program to "paint" the letters, S-T-O-P. The heat treatment to seal the paint. The fasteners to bolt the sign to the pole. The hole digger to put it in the ground. The reflectors around the edge. The solar panel fixed to the top of the sign to make LED lights blink a flashing red. It boggled my mind just realizing everything that went into making a stop sign. A stop sign! Something we've all seen a million times. You see it. You tap the brakes. You pause a second, look to your right to see if there's someone else at the intersection, and then you go on with your day. And yet, there's so much more to it.

Stop signs are funny like that. You never think about them, and there's so much more to them.

They keep order in a neighborhood. They provide a landing area for birds, a target for snowballs, or a trigger for memories.

As soon as a new stop sign is added to a familiar area that never had one before, you may as well have painted that thing with purple polka-dots. There's a stop sign at the end of my parents' street, before you turn onto another street, with another stop sign about 100 yards away. This stop sign came to the neighborhood about 20 years after my parents moved in. So, it of course is optional in their minds. It has never caused a problem, it's just funny how the mind works. That's the NEW stop sign, I was fine without it. I'll be fine now, too.

And of course there's my favorite ever stop sign. The stop sign at the three-way stop at the corner of Orchard and Plomondon in Wheaton. This sign was the one my brother and I would pass each morning on our way to caddy at Chicago Golf Club. The sign itself was pretty standard, but someone had added a sticker that said "Eating" below the word stop. So, of course, now the sign read, "STOP Eating." And of course, every day, my brother Patrick would say in his best monotone, "STOPPPP Eaaaaaating." And every morning I would smile. To this day, I can't go a week without thinking, "Stop Eating!"

And you know what, someone had to invent the printing process, and the adhesive to stick that eating sticker to the stop sign in the first place. And man, am I glad they did!

Floor Mat Technology

T here are quite a few good indicators that illustrate just how much things in life change over the course of many years. Electronics are always a great example. TVs. Computers. Cell phones are hilarious to look back on in movies and TV shows and see just how drastically things can change. Some movies are good about not putting in too many pieces of footage that date the movie, and others are chock-full of flip phones and VCRs.

Hair and clothing styles are of course another great one. Having watched way too many bad Eighties movies from the free OnDemand section of my cable subscription, it still gets me when I see some classic Eighties hair or an actor wearing some super-thick rimmed glasses in any movie from 1991 to 1994.

Recently, I noticed something far less obvious that showed me just how far we'd come in the last ten years as a society. Floor mat technology in cars!

Have you seen some of the new bells and whistles these new car floor mats have these days? I'm in awe.

My first car was a 2002 Chevy Monte Carlo. It was black, and to me, it had floor mats. They too were black, and there really wasn't much to them. They had sort of a fuzzy carpet feel to them, and they had a little bit of tread on the bottom to keep them in place. Except that didn't work. After about two weeks, the tread was almost completely worn out, and the fuzzy fabric was filled with gravel, dirt and dust. By the time fall rolled around, there were leaves under the mats, they were permanently soggy from rain, and later snow.

I drove that Monte Carlo for nine years. After the first few months, I really didn't notice the floor mats. They were awful. I knew this. They probably knew this. We had a mutual understanding for each other's shortcomings. I continued to track in dirt and precipitation, and they continued not to be able to handle it.

In July 2011, the Monte was done in by an accident that left him totaled. It was quite tough to say goodbye to a good friend. My first car. The only car my mom will ever demand I stand next to and get a picture with.

But...at least I was able to move on to a bright world that exposed me to so much more in terms of floor mat technology.

Soon after Monte bit the dust, I acquired a 2006 Mini Cooper. Mini Coopers are one of those things that are a lot like an innovative European juicer system you might buy on an infomercial. They seem so inviting from afar. They look different. They seem fun. Everyone who has one raves about it...And then you buy one...

And immediately you realize, "This thing is small. This thing doesn't handle that well. This thing is very expensive to repair. This thing takes premium gas. Heck, I barely fit in this thing, and just to fit in it, I have to scrunch down and sacrifice my posture..."

However, MINIs have AMAZING floor mats. At least for what I was used to. They are made with a fabric material that appears as though to have some sort of water resistant treatment to it. The fabric is sealed, not fuzzy, and repels water and dirt. Near the area of the driver's mat where the heel is most likely to hit, there is a reinforced pad that has been strategically positioned to keep your heel from wearing a hole in the mat. The contour of the cabin of the car was erected in such a way that the mats stayed in place much better than the Monte. There was minimal mat slippage, and it was fantastic. When dirt and gravel entered the car, they were easily just brushed off the mat, and out the door.

In the long run though, the floor mats couldn't save the Mini. After nearly two years of costly repairs, expensive gas, multiple compressed vertebrae, and far too many middle aged women telling me the Mini was "cute," I cut ties with the old Mini Wheat.

And as I moved on, I continued to move up in terms of floor mat technology. My new car is a Chevy Malibu. It's a 2013, and boy has floor mat technology come a long way in the last seven years. The Mini was new to me, but even when I got it, its floor mats were five years old. It's night and day in new cars these days. My new car has a fitted plastic button at the bottom corner of each of the front seat foot landing areas. In a stroke of genius, these buttons connect in with the floor mat itself to keep it locked in place, no matter how much jostling the mats have to take from feet, water, leaves, sand, you name it.

As soon as I realized the genius of this invention, I started to see it everywhere. On my last rental car, sure enough, fitted buttons. On my mom's car, fitted buttons. It's like a revolution is happening right before my eyes.

I can sit very firmly in my seat, dig my heels into the mat, and it doesn't even think about budging. Do you know how amazing a feeling that is? It's unreal.

It's amazing to think in ten years' time, something as seemingly insignificant as a floor mat has changed so much for the better. So cool!

Free Food Tastes Better

I'm not sure why it is, but people seem to LOVE free food. And not only do they love it, but it sure seems like they are way more open-minded about trying it, eating more of it, or talking about it with their friends.

I was at a work event this week, and I had a chance to see this behavior in action, yet again.

The host of our event informed us that there was some leftover turkey sandwiches and pesto pasta from an event earlier that day. It was around dinner time, so you can imagine that people's ears would perk up a little bit. But my goodness, you would have thought someone just announced that Gordon Ramsay was going to personally marinate this turkey, cut it, and prepare the world's best ever turkey sandwich. Don't get me wrong, the turkey sandwich is a fine meal item of which I've probably consumed 300 or so in my lifetime. But really people? If someone had said they were going to run over to the local convenient store, and asked if anyone wanted a turkey sandwich, I'm guessing there might have been some orders for roller hot dogs before someone sought out a turkey sandwich.

As they waited for our turkey sandwiches to arrive (I did not order one), the anticipation continued to grow amongst the group.

"Man, I LOVE turkey sandwiches!" one guy brimmed with excitement.

"I've been craving a turkey sandwich all day!" said another lady.

I couldn't believe it. I'm not a psychologist, and I'm sure there is some phenomenon to describe what happens when people are presented with an unexpected gift and the reaction that triggers in their minds, but this was unbelievable.

I suppose it's possible that the guy who LOVED turkey sandwiches really LOVED turkey sandwiches so much that he was just ready to go off at any mention of them. And I know it's also possible that the lady was actually craving a turkey sandwich all day long, but how much of this is tied to the fact that all the sudden they were unexpectedly given the option out of nowhere?

My guess, it had a lot to do with it.

The pesto pasta that came along with the turkey sandwiches looked frightening. It was like stuffed pasta in a murky green sauce. It kind of looked like algae. And yet, the group seemed to gobble it up as if they were an army of frogs. Maybe they were all being polite, maybe they all really like pesto, but this certainly seemed like the type of thing that if there had been a big bowl of it on Thanksgiving at grandma's house, not a soul would have touched it. As people were scarfing it down, the expressions on their faces went from surprised, to accepting, to enjoying with each bite. As if they were saying, "Okay, that's kind of funky tasting" to "Alright, that's not awful" to "Hey, that was free!"

The final illustration of this phenomenon in action was with the dessert plate that night. There was a pretty nice spread of cookies, brownies, fruit bars, etc. There were chocolate chip cookies, raisin cookies, peanut butter cookies, frosted brownies, fudge brownies, chocolate chip brownies…and these crazy looking fruit-nut-date bars. You know where this is going…

Why out of that spread anyone would choose to eat a fruit-nut-date bar I cannot fathom. And yet, nearly everyone in the group had one. And raved about it. I realize that maybe I shouldn't be shocked at this point, considering this was the same group of people that had just applauded turkey sandwiches like they were prime rib, and gladly eaten algae pesto pasta, but I couldn't believe it.

There has to be more to this. It's almost as if since you would be much less likely to seek out a fruit-nut-date bar, the fact that it was there and free for the taking that it became that much more attractive. I do have to say, it was fun to watch people enjoy their turkey sandwiches. All reasons aside, everyone enjoyed their dinner.

After everyone had already eaten, I got up and helped myself to a turkey sandwich.

It was the best turkey sandwich I've ever had.

Life is a Special Occasion

I write cliché marketing messages for a living. At least four times a year, I tell people not to miss the sale of the year! Shop now and get our best deals of the season, and then three weeks later, make sure not to miss the sale so big you can't afford to miss! As you might imagine, this has a way of turning me into a skeptic when it comes to fully buying into the fluffy marketing messaging that other companies use to try and prompt me to buy things. Throughout the course of history, no company has done more of this than Hallmark.

While from a business side of things, I respect anyone that can turn Secretary's Day...oh wait, Administrative Professional's Day...into a way to sell more cards and flowers, I have to admit I've never really liked Hallmark (Author's Note: In case you were wondering, Administrative Professional's Day is the Wednesday of the last full week of April each year. Mark your calendar!).

To a cynic, Hallmark is nothing more than a paper company that uses the emotional heartstrings of consumers to extract money from their wallets and sell cards for any ridiculous occasion. Up until this week, I was that cynic. Until, I saw what I may have previously thought was a super corny gift bag. I had always thought of Hallmark Holidays as ridiculous occasions. But, what if I had thought of them as special occasions?

The bag that I saw simply said "Life is a Special Occasion." The me of two days ago might have thought, "Gag! Come on Hallmark, that's one of your best ploys yet! Life is a Special Occasion? Okay...Good one!"

But the more I thought about it, the more I thought, "Why not?'"

Why not treat life as if all of it were a series of special occasions? What does it really hurt? In today's fast-paced, attention-seeking lifestyle that celebrity culture seems to try and force on all of us, social norms plead with us to make everything a big deal. Every weekend has to be filled with occasions so special we can all post 68 pictures on Facebook, and tag all of our friends on Instagram. If we aren't front row at a big concert, or on the 50 yard line at the football game, it's as if we aren't living at all. In the quest for those special occasions, nothing seems to be special

Joe Montana.

Why not embrace the Hallmark approach? Why not send someone a card on the third Thursday of every other month? Or, better yet just call them, or not be afraid to go to the local high school football game and post a picture of the crowd of 107 that is enjoying the game? It's not prestigious. It's not awe-inspiring. But it's life. That in-itself is special.

Seeing old ladies at the grocery store who walk so slow you're positive their half gallon of milk is going to go bad well before they get out to their old Buick, let alone back to their house. Seeing little kids run around in public making airplane noises while their Velcro shoes almost fly off their feet.

Watching an Army patrolman carry around his daughter while she plays with the patch on the shoulder of his uniform.

These are special occasions. They might not go on Facebook, and there's not a photo filter on Instagram that can capture the full emotion of that little girl's face, but they are what's real about life. They are what's special.

Leave it to Hallmark to remind me of this fact. Maybe that corny marketing copy does work after all...

The Crutches in the Garage

Certain things happen in life that we really don't understand. Maybe we're not meant to understand them yet, or maybe their importance cannot be fully understood at the time. Even harder is when those things that happen in life that give us our perspective don't even happen to us. As the person learning the lesson, it's hard to know which things we're supposed be learning from—since they may be quite indirect. And as the person whose life event serves as a tool from which someone else

may learn, it can extremely difficult to accept that something difficult will end up benefitting someone in the future. Maybe you,
maybe someone else.

I've had a tremendous example of this in my life, and for almost
40 years, my father has paid the price so I could reap the reward.
My father was involved in a car accident in 1976. The severity of
the accident nearly killed him, broke both of his legs, feet and
countless other bones. From what I've heard, it was beyond
horrific. To this day one of his legs is shorter than the other, he's
had to have his knee replaced, and still walks around with a
bunch of screws and staples in his left leg. Watching him walk
through an airport metal detector is almost comical.

Growing up, I didn't think much of this. Sure, my dad couldn't
really run, we didn't ever go skiing as a family, and I'd never been
on water skis until I was in my twenties, but to me it was never an
issue. We played catch together. When I was a pitcher growing
up, he couldn't squat to catch, so he sat in a chair. If I missed the
chair, I had to run and get the ball. We didn't treat it as his
limitation, we treated it as a teaching moment for me: Don't make
wild throws.

The thing I remember most about growing up with my dad
were the things he didn't say. The excuses he didn't make. The
complaints I never heard. We all knew he was in pain all the time.
It was excruciatingly obvious, but he didn't let it become something that defined him. There were times I wish we went skiing as
a family, or that maybe we all would have learned how to water
ski. Of course, he never said we couldn't, but it was one of those
things where if we had time together, we tried to pick activities
that everyone could participate in. I'll gladly sacrifice the ability
to ski for the memories I had growing up. And who knows, maybe
I'll still learn some day.

Every once in a while, the bad legs still give Pops problems.
The knee will act up. The hip will be thrown off somehow. That
darn sciatic nerve will send pain shooting every direction. He'll
let you know it hurts, but he won't complain.

For most of my life a set of crutches have never been far off.
When I was a kid, they spent most of their time in the attic, their

services not needed as often. But, as I've gotten older, they've made more and more appearances to help out.

I spent a week at home recently and saw the crutches in the garage right next to the stoop that leads out of the house. A sure sign that not too long ago their assistance must have been needed. I know the pain. I've seen it time and time again. But it's never the focus. It never slows my father down. He may move slower, but it never stops him. He's used those crutches at work, he's used those crutches doing chores around the house, you name it. Heck many times, the lawn mower is as much of a crutch as they are.

When I see those crutches, I think sacrifice. I think of all the times my father was in pain, and never complained. I think about all the times I sure he wanted to. All the times he wanted to call into work and take a day off, and didn't. All the times he wanted to feel sorry for himself for having to spend the majority of his life as a physical mess. But that's not who he is.

I worked long hours last week when I was home. I didn't get a lot of sleep, and I was generally irritable. But seeing those crutches in the garage, and knowing what pain and sacrifice are really like, I kept my mouth shut. I had one long week. My feet were a little sore. Big deal. Let's see how I feel in forty years after someone broke most of the bones in my body...Maybe then I'll complain.

Actually, no I won't. Pops taught me better than that.

Made-Up Words

Most people who know me have probably heard me make up a word or two over the course of time. What can I say, it happens. The Oxford Dictionary estimates that there are somewhere around a quarter of a million English words. Even they can't accurately count how many variations and plurals of words there are. There are just so many words!

Well, if I had my say, there'd be a lot more of them, too.

Making up words is so much fun.

The other day I found myself just saying the word Nargle-muffin, over and over again. Narglemuffin.

Yes, I know, this makes little to no sense at all.

What is Nargle? Luna Lovegood may think a Nargle is one thing, but since I'm one of the six people on earth not to have read Harry Potter, I don't think this influenced me. So what did?

I don't even know. I don't even know what Nargle rhymes with. To clarify, I say "nar-gull" when I spell Nargle. I suppose it doesn't have to be a capital letter, but hey, I made up the word, I can do whatever I want.

There is definitely a formula for how these words make it into my own personal lexicon. This particular one has its roots in the word Darge (Of course, it does.).

You see, I really don't believe in using curse words. So, in the event that there may be a word that might be getting close to something like that, I do a quick switcheroo.

Darge was born from darn. You say darn enough, and it just gets Darge boring. So by comparison, Darge is way more appealing. It's much more satisfying.

Darge!

So Darge had a pretty good run, but over time, even that one got worn out. Aww, darrrge. When you start elongating the R's, that's usually a pretty good sign that the word is on its way out.

This made way to Nargle, which is actually quite logical, if you think about it. When Darge got long and drawn out, it became darrrrge, and the antidote to such things is a very quick, abrupt R sound. In fact, when Nargle started, it was so quick, and so sudden, it was actually probably closer to Nrgle. You know, with no A.

This became a great way to express displeasure with things. You stub your toe, NARGLE. You drop a carton of strawberries in the parking lot at the grocery store, Nargle! You run into someone at a stadium and they drop their order of chicken tenders, "Nar— Oh my gosh, sorry." It's times like these that Nargle doesn't actually work. You pull that one out, and the guy looks at you funny like, uh, what is Nargle? Buy me some more food, BRO.

But, to tell you the truth, I have no idea what to say about Narglemuffin. It's fun to say, although I'm not sure you want to eat one... In fact, I think I better go buy some chicken tenders. Those sound good right about now!

Oh, Save It!

I can't really yo-yo at all. I never really could. There was a phase in my life, I think it might have been around middle school age, where yo-yos made a comeback. There were all of these different variations of stalling models that allowed the user to basically unravel the yo-yo, and it would stall down at the bottom of the string. The yo-yo operator would then attempt to hold the string in such a manner to perform tricks with the yo-yo. Walk the dog, cat's cradle, all sorts of things I can't even remember at this point.

All I know is that it didn't matter how fancy the yo-yo, I couldn't yo-yo.

I'm pretty sure a family member got me one of the fancy ones many years ago, and I proceeded to be the only kid in the seventh grade who couldn't stall an automatically stalling yo-yo. I not even sure that's possible, but seventh grade me found a way not to be able to do it.

I'm not sure what happened to that yo-yo. Hopefully I gave it to someone who could actually benefit from its perceived awesomeness. I wouldn't know because it was never awesome to me....But I'm sure it was pretty sweet to someone who knew how to wield it correctly.

However, I do have a very plain green plastic yo-yo. And for the life of me, I don't know why. I don't ever recall receiving this yo-yo, and Lord knows I've never been able to use it. So why on Earth do I have it?

What's even more ridiculous is that I specifically remember moving this yo-yo two different times. First, when I moved out of my parents' house after college, and then again when I relocated to Nashville a few years later. Granted, it was in the same desk each time, and it hasn't moved in years, but it got me thinking about saving things.

I'm not a hoarder. Every so often I purge a lot of items when things get too cluttered. I do love things with sentimental value, so I could see saving things like that as a reason why I might end up with an item like this green yo-yo. But honestly, I'm not sure I've ever used this thing. Well, I know I haven't, because I can't. But I'm not even sure anyone has. And who knows how long I've had it. The string is yellowing, so it must be a while...

Why do I have this thing?

It does me no good. I keep it in the drawer where I keep my extra pencils, markers and crayons. I go in that drawer like twice a year, tops!

It's crazy to think this thing has moved with me 500 miles from Chicago to Nashville, while providing me absolutely no value.

Here's my theory. Certain things are just hard to throw away. Like a screw. Everyone has a coffee can full of loose screws, or bolts, or something. It's just one of those things, who would ever think to themselves, you know what, I think I have enough screws? IT NEVER HAPPENS.

Water bottles are the same way. If you're the athletic type of person who uses water bottles, you're probably also the type of person that gets a lot of free water bottles. From races, corporate outings, kid's sporting events, whatever the case may be. A 37-cent free water bottle with a logo on it is one of the easiest things in the world to give out. And, as long as it's not moldy, cracked or the lid doesn't stay on, one of the hardest things to throw away. Honey, do you want me to throw away that free water bottle? Of course not. You're going to save it for nine years until a spider lays eggs in it, at which time you will then throw it away having never used it. It's like a fact of life.

Half the time the logo on the water bottle is ugly, obsolete, or peels off within a week or two. Doesn't matter. You'll keep it.

Other examples of this phenomenon include kids play toys, a commemorative program from pretty much anything as important as a piano recital on up to a college commencement, pot holders (no holes of course), and unripped blankets or afghans.

My bet is that you could pretty much go into any house in America and ask them when the last time they threw out a non-ripped blanket, you'll get a lot of nevers as your answers.

I mean, why would you? A blanket is a blanket. As long as it doesn't have a hole in it or wasn't tattered by the dog, there's really no reason to get rid of it. And even in that case, you can use it to make a bunch of rags, or line the trunk of your car.

Even for the people in life who can't stand saving anything, there are a multitude of items that you just don't throw away. But that brings me back to the green yo-yo.

I suppose maybe I would feel bad just throwing it away, knowing that it's a toy, and that it works just fine, and that some kid somewhere would probably want it. Potentially the fact that it's heavy plastic, and will make a loud thud in my trash can is something that I've been avoiding...

However, even after all these years, I have no sentimental value for this yo-yo. I have no functional value for this yo-yo. It serves me no purpose whatsoever, so I think it's time to go.

Does anyone want a green yo-yo?

There's no way I'm going to be able to throw it away!

Old People Names

My brother coaches freshmen soccer at a high school outside St. Louis, and he tells me a lot of stories about kids named Jordan, Grant, Junior—I can't remember all the rest, but it's safe to say that all of the names are pretty contemporary sounding. I have cousins, and other friends with younger kids named Tanner, Austin, Madison, Sydney, Breeanne. The list could go on and on. You hear a lot of names out there, but there are just some names you NEVER hear.

Helga. Ethel. Beverly. Mildred. Virgil. Mortimer. Velma. Gertrude.

What happened to these names?

You hear names like this, and immediately you think of someone's great aunt. Ahhh yes, Great Aunt Bernice. Or Grandpa Virgil.

Seriously, does anyone know anyone under the age of ninety named Ethel?

Can you even imagine a first grader walking into school and announcing to the class, "Hi, my name is Ethel!"

I've got to think that most of the kids would look at each other and think, "What's an 'Ethel?'"

The words, "Virgil, do you want to play with your Transformers?" have probably never been spoken in the same sentence in the history of time. Unless some nursing home worker somewhere asked 92 year-old Virgil if he wanted to play with some of the transformers that used to operate his old Lionel train set.

What it is about some names that allow them to transcend generations, while others go the way of Henrietta or Maude?

Does it have to do with fame or notoriety? Joan of Arc might be a good example of that one. She was born in 1412, and yet Joan, and the French translation of her name, Jean, are still widely used today.

Or maybe it's all about the Bible. Biblical names like Peter, Mark, John, Daniel, those never seem to go out of style.

Possibly there's a presidential connection in America. Thomas, James, William...

But then there are exceptions to all of these rules.

King Arthur was a pretty prominent fellow in medieval times, yet there aren't a whole lot of little Arthur's running around now are there?

Job was the subject of a pretty famous biblical story, and outside of Jobe on "Arrested Development," how many others of those have there been?

For every Thomas, James and William we get with presidential lineage, there are a lot more we don't get. Chester A. Arthur? Where's the love for old Chet? Grover Cleveland? Good enough for "Sesame Street" but not for any real kids. And for the love of all that is holy, has there ever been another Millard after Millard Fillmore?

You would think with all of the kids being born these days, we could get a Cornelius or a Miriam.

I mean, I've got to admit, some of the names sound dated, and probably not the most attractive, but then again, neither is Steve, and yet that's a Top 115 name on the Social Security Administration's database of most popular names for 2013.

Fred by contrast—poor Fred—is the 819th most popular boy's name in 2013. One hundred years ago, Fred ranked 27th.

Mildred ranked sixth in 1913, and spent the next three years in the top 10 every year. Now old Aunt Millie hasn't even cracked the top 1000 since 1984! What happened? Was every girl named Mildred just a bad little girl to the point where all the other moms in the neighborhood swore that their next kid was NOT going to be a Mildred, until eventually there were none left?

There may be hope at the end of all of this for some names. A hundred years ago, Noah, a name steeped in Biblical tradition, and with a nice sound to it, was mired in 348th place for boys born in 1913. Fifty years later by 1963, poor Noah had plummeted to an all-time low 693rd position. But, as fate would have it, the ark builder is on his way back. Noah has been in the top 50 every year since 1996, and in 2013 he's marched all the way to No. 4!

Perhaps there are other bright days ahead for other names too. Isaiah has climbed from 204th in 1993 to 42nd today. And Rose might be on the comeback as well, having jumped 80 spots in the last two years.

There are certainly cultural events that lead to the popularity of names. Ingrid Bergman, the Hollywood starlet of the 1940s propelled her namesake from outside of the top 1000 in 1939 to 461 in 1947. She just happened to win an Oscar, a Tony and two Golden Globes during this time frame.

Peyton Manning may be singularly responsible for popularizing his name, for both boys and girls. It never even appeared on either a boy or girl name top 1000 list prior to 1989 and only started to in the mid-Nineties when he arrived on the scene as a prominent quarterback. The name has since cracked, and continued to hover around the top 150 for both boys, and girls for the last 18 years. Not bad for old #18...

Growing up, I always loved odd names. Matthew has been in the top 16 names for every year out of the last 40, so there have always been plenty of Matts, and this always bothered me. In one class, I think there were three of us, and I became Matt T. At one point in Cub Scouts, there were six Matts in our troop, and I was actually referred to as Matt 5, or Matt 6, I can't remember which. Talk about feeling special!

I have no idea if I'll have a kid one day, and I'm sure if I do, there will be some thought about using good old family names like Daniel or John. But Lord knows, I'd love to help start the revival for the name Fred, or Grover! Grover is such an awesome name.

Some people may not like the sounds of it, but I could definitely get used to going into a room every night, tucking a little girl in, reading her a story, and saying, Goodnight, I love you, Ethel!

Loving Google but Hating the Yankees

hree days are especially sweet to most of the baseball world each year. Opening Day, the day your team wins the World Series, and the day that the Yankees get eliminated from contention. As I write this, today marked just the second time in the last 19 years the Yankees were eliminated from contention without qualifying for the playoffs. A season marred with injuries up and down the lineup and an inconsistent pitching staff, it was a wonder the Yanks even contended at all.

However, this story isn't about baseball. It's about a shared hatred for the institution of the Yankees. A hatred that is so universal, yet so misguided, it's nearly ridiculous.

Let's leave the baseball diamond for a second and head on over into Silicon Valley, a mere 2950 miles from Yankee Stadium (a 41-hour drive if you must know). There sits what is simple known to the tech world as the Googleplex.

In the fifteen years since Google's founding, Surgey Brin, Larry Page, and now Eric Schmidt have turned what started out as a search engine into one of the world's most respected companies. Google dominates its core business, search traffic, is routinely voted as one of the best places to work, hires top talent, treats its employees well, invests in the communities it serves, and does it all with a benevolence that is summed up by the company mantra of "Do No Evil."

Google has become so synonymous with searching the Internet that it has become a verb in the English language, its logo is one of the most simplistic, yet most recognizable in the world, and aside from some fanatics & contrarians, Google really has very few public haters. And oh by the way, Google makes a LOT of money.

In 2012, the Goog turned $50 billion in revenue into $10 billion in profit, and currently has assets nearing $100 billion.

Just reading all of that is remarkable, and to think they did it all in 15 years. If Google isn't the latest definition of the realization of the American success, what is?

Now let's look at the New York Yankees.

Baseball's most dominant team in history. Owners of 27 World Series titles, 40 American League pennants, and nearly every meaningful record for winning in American sports history. The Yankees play in the most state-of-the-art facility in baseball, they pay their players more than any team in baseball, sell more merchandise than any team in baseball, and are the most popular team in America's most popular city. To boot, the Yankees have featured some of the most recognizable players in the history of sport. Babe Ruth, Lou Gehrig, Joe Dimaggio, Yogi Berra, Mickey Mantle, Mariano Rivera, and the current face of the franchise, Derek Jeter.

In 1973, the Yankees were purchased for $8.7 million dollars. In the last 40 years, the team has capitalized on success, history, and its position as a global icon to turn their net worth into an estimated $2.3 billion in 2013. Not bad for a bunch of ballplayers.

Oh, and one more thing I forgot to mention. The iconic NY logo on Yankees hats and jerseys, it was designed by Tiffany's. Yes, that Tiffany's.

And yet, somehow, the Yankees are the most hated team in sports. If you're not a Yankee fan, there's a good chance you're a Yankee hater.

"The Yankees suck. They always win, but they just buy the best players, spend the most money, they have their own TV station, in the biggest market, and they just make more money than everyone else. What the Yankees do isn't really winning, it's almost cheating. That's not what sports is supposed to be."

I'm not sure this is a direct quote, but if you were to summarize all of the sentiment on the Internet, around sports bars, and around office water coolers, that's pretty much what you'd hear. Let's think about the above statement, as it applies to Google.

"Google is awesome. They have the best products, they hire the best talent, and spend the most money to ensure that talent stays happy. They created their own market, they have their head-quarters right in the heart of their industry, and make billions of dollars every year. Year after year, Google keeps finding more and more ways to get better at what they do. It isn't just winning, it's the definition of success."

Looking at the two statements, they are nearly identical. Again, this was a convenient paraphrase of public sentiment about Google, but the point is clear.

Google and the Yankees are pretty similar.

One could argue on a few points.

Google is only 15 years old, and has only recently become a world power. Some might say they are still in the honeymoon stage of their success, and thus have yet to wear down the public perception that goes along with other entities that are just too good, for too long. The Yankees have been a consistent winner for more than 80 years.

It is interesting to note that a company like GE has also been a titan for a hundred years, and people don't seem to hate them...But back to Google.

The other argument point for Google as to why they are so much more revered in the public's eye is the "Do No Evil" mantra. For years Google has operated under this credo as a way to as-sure the public that despite the huge amounts of data and personal information that they possess about so many Americans, it is said to be their number one priority is to never do anything that isn't in the public's best interest. Whether you believe this is another issue, but at least in the public spotlight that's what they've always said. And, from the looks of it, America trusts them.

The Yankees on the other hand are more than casually referred to as "The Evil Empire." The Star Wars reference has grown into their unofficial moniker more and more over the last twenty years. Over this same time frame, the Yankees have outspent, outwon, and outearned every other team in baseball, and it isn't even close.

Yet, why are they so evil? Over the last twenty years, they have been managed by Joe Torre, and Joe Girardi—two of the most respected men in their field. The Yankees teams have been led by Derek Jeter and Mariano Rivera, two embodiments of class in the modern athlete. Ambassadors to the city, they are global icons.

One name has been conspicuously missing from this argument, and that name is Steinbrenner. As in George Steinbrenner. For 37 years, from 1973 until his death in 2010, "The Boss" ran the Yankees with an iron fist, and an uncompromising will. He was brash, and he was brazen, and he rocked the old boys club that was Major League Baseball ownership like no one before him.

But was he really evil?

He rescued baseball's proudest franchise from near bankruptcy in 1973, turned them into a winner within four years, won seven championships in total, renovated Yankee Stadium, and later built an all new state-of-the-art stadium for the next 50 years of success. He changed the way a baseball team made money off its merchandise, and its brand. He changed the landscape of sports media with the creation of the YES Network, a model that is being copied across the country. The man was a true innovator.

Most people's biggest problem with the man is the conception that he used his wealth and his position to simply buy his way to the top.

Hmmm, WWGD? (What Would Google Do?)

Would Google simply let Microsoft, or Facebook, or Apple have all of the best assets in their industry without making a serious play to control them themselves?

Would Google make $50 billion and not invest it in their future success?

Would Google not capitalize on its position as a market leader to continue to set themselves up for future success in the years to come?

Of course not.

In 2006, Google shelled out $1.65 billion to buy YouTube. Did you hear anybody say, "Oh come on! Google is cheating, they just spent $1.6 billion on YouTube!"

Of course not, and at the same time, as the search giant got even stronger, and created more revenue sources for ads, you didn't hear anyone crying foul because Ask Jeeves never stood a chance.

I'm sure if you asked any executive in Silicon Valley, they'd relish the opportunity to go toe-to-toe with Google. To learn from them, to be pushed by them. Millions of entrepreneurs try each year to show up on Google's radar. To challenge them, and ultimately to hopefully be purchased by them. In the end, Google's value and strength in the market drives up the value for all of the companies that operate in their shadow. Those billion dollar valuations wouldn't be what they are if someone wasn't willing to pay them. The exact same way major league baseball players wouldn't make the kind of money they do if there weren't teams like the Yankees willing to pay their salaries.

The Yankees may be the most valuable franchise with a net worth of $2.3 billion, but the average MLB franchise is worth more than $700 million. Like Google, the Yankees have grown the game for every franchise, and they spurred competition from every other team to put a better product on the field, to provide better media coverage off of it, and create a fan experience that rivals that of what you'll find in the Bronx.

If you're a fan of progress, chances are you're a fan of Google. If you're a fan of baseball, you really should love the Yankees.

Writing Letters, Spell Check, and the Expansion of Our Vocabulary

Not too many people actually handwrite letters anymore. It's a shame really. There's something about sitting down with a nice pen and actually having to meticulously plan out what you're going to say. Then, you have to carefully craft your words so they fit evenly across the space allowed by the width of your writing surface. Writing by hand, you don't have the luxury of automatic line breaks or the perfect line spacing you get on a computer, or even a typewriter for that matter.

There's something so much more personal about a handwritten letter. Knowing that the author had to actually sit down, stop what they were doing and singularly focus on the task of writing out the letter. It's not like an email where you know they very easily could have been written out while riding the train, or during a dull moment in the office, or over the course of multiple sessions of who knows what.

Writing a letter on the other hand is an event. You sit down somewhere specific to write a letter. You may put music on in the background, and you may have a calming beverage to accompany you, but other than that, with a letter, it's just the author and their words.

I think the fact that our society as a whole doesn't really write letters anymore reflects in more ways than we realize. It's way too easy to fire off an email in the heat of the moment. We often say the first things that come to mind, and hit SEND before we even realize what we've said. Or we spout off anonymously on message boards or forums where the shroud of anonymity gives people the ability to say nearly anything without having to actually own their comments. With a letter, you have to go through the process of actually writing it out, putting it in an envelope, buying a stamp and getting it in the mail. If at any point in that process your emotions were to stabilize, the chances of an ill-timed letter being sent are much less than the heat of the moment that can often get the best of us over email.

Having access to such quick means of communication has diminished our collective patience as a society. Even as recently as 50 years ago, you had to write a letter, send a telegram, or pay for a long distance call to communicate with someone in the next state over. If the situation was emotionally charged, you waited. Patience got the better part of valor. In today's society, we write nasty emails, spout off snarky replies, and hide behind the safety of our computer screens or smart phones.

However, all is not lost. One great thing has come from the digital letter writing era that actually may be advancing our society.

SPELL CHECK.

Now before you tell me that we've had dictionaries for years, let me explain.

It's not so much that spell check allows us to send letters without spelling errors, it's the fact that spell check lets writers write, without the hesitation that comes with spelling uncertainty.

It may have been a while since you actually wrote a handwritten letter and ran into this problem. So let me refresh you.

You're writing a thank you note to your Great Aunt Jeanine. Because her name is Jeanine, we already know she was born before the age of electronic communication, and thus this thank you note is written on a foldable paper note card.

Aunt J has just bestowed upon you a not-so-crispy five dollar bill for your birthday and told you not to spend Old Abe all in one place. At the request of your mother, your thank you note must be thoughtful, well-penned, and at least five sentences long. This is the only time you'll talk to her all year, and she's on a fixed income, so those five dollars should mean a lot to you...The least you can do is write a thoughtful note.

Ambitiously, you sit down and start to think up meaningful sentences to thank your great aunt for the five dollars. And almost immediately, you find yourself needing spell check:

Dear Aunt Jeanine,

Thank you so much for thinking of me on my birthday. I can't tell you how apprec...

How do you spell appreciative? Ehhh, I'm not exactly sure...Let's not say that word, it's a tough one...

Dear Aunt Jeanine,

Thank you so much for thinking of me on my birthday. I recieved....

Cripes, it's I before e, EXCEPT after C... Cross it out? White it out? Keep going with it mis-spelled? Where's my bottle of white out? It's all dried up and crusty. Ugh...

Dear Aunt Jeanine,

Thank you so much for thinking of me on my birthday. Your card came in the mail, and I inadvert...

Not again...How do you spell inadvertently? Why am I even trying to use big words???

Dear Aunt Jeanine,

Thank you for the birthday card. Thank you very much for the five dollars. I'll be sure to put it in the bank soon. I almost threw it in the garbage when I got it by accident. I'm glad I didn't.

Thanks again,

Matt

There you have it. No misspelled words. No confusion. No problem.

But also no emotion, for crying out loud. Why send the note in the first place? If that thing doesn't scream, Dear Aunt Jeanine, Mom made me send this note, what would?

But there is an answer to this, and it is spell check. One of the truly useful inventions to come around in the last 25 years.

You can be as verbose as you want with old Aunt Jeanine, and the little red squiggly line underneath your poorly spelled words is just a click away from being fixed. No anxiety. No sweat, and hopefully more emotion:

Salutations (corrected) to the third most influential septuagenarian (corrected) in my life,

It is with an immense level of gratitude with which I would like to recognize (corrected) your supreme level of generosity (corrected) with regards to the anniversary of my birth. It was with great pleasure that I was able to successfully extract the five dollar treasury (corrected) note from your expertly sealed envelope. I look forward to corresponding (corrected) again soon.

Alright, so maybe that's a bit much, but the main point is that spell check allows the writer to take risks they wouldn't normally take if they were writing on paper.

Welcome to Club Honk

I 'm not that old. Some days I feel older than I am, but let's face it, I'm not that old. But I have been driving for quite a while. Again, not as long as some people, but by my best estimation, probably somewhere around 130,000 miles. Long enough to have seen some things happen on the road, that's for sure.

I once saw a guy run head on into another car at an intersection and literally fly through the windshield of his car, land, roll over, and walk away with only a small cut (He should probably look into being a stuntman).

I was once following a flatbed truck down I-75 while it was carrying the type of drainage pipe that goes in a roadside ditch. You know, the one that has a diameter of about eight feet. It rolled right off the truck, and bounded down the road. Talk about unexpected. Luckily no one was hurt.

I was once following a farm truck that was transporting about a hundred chickens. Traveling at about 75 miles an hour, one of the chickens escaped. That didn't end well.

I once drove the wrong way on to an off ramp for I-40 in Arizona. I've also turned the wrong way down a one-way street and almost gotten flattened by a moving van...On Music Row in Nashville no less.

I've driven Corvettes, Hummers, trucks of all kinds. Pulled trailers, and yes, even owned a Mini Cooper as well.

But today, I did something while driving a car that I'd never done before.

I honked the horn.

Mind you, I've honked the horn many a time to tell people that I have arrived to pick them up, or bid them farewell, and to acknowledge that I'm seeing someone on the road that I know.

But before today, I'd never used the horn as an alert mechanism to tell another motorist that I'm in the area, that I want them to do something, or to even to express displeasure.

I've sat in my parents' driveway laying on the horn in disgust that the garage door wasn't working and I was locked out of the house...

But I'd never used the horn for the cautionary purposes for which it was invented.

Innocently enough, I was stopping at Target to pick up a bunch of bananas and some chicken breasts, when a red Honda Pilot started to slowly back out of its parking spot and toward the path of my car. It was dark, but I saw its back up lights. Without thinking, I pressed my horn. A sound came out, and the Pilot stopped. The horn blow was not loud, and the Honda didn't slam on the brakes. It simply stopped. I continued on, and about three parking spaces later I parked my car.

It wasn't really a close call. The Pilot has just started to back up, and I was still a few spots away when I had honked. As I was sitting in the parking space, my heart wasn't racing, but I was still kind of in shock.

I had just honked my horn. How did I know to do that? I'd never done it before, and I've been in plenty of situation where I probably should have! And yet for some reason, tonight, at Target, I had done it. I felt great!

And not even great in the sense that I had just blasted this person for being unaware. I hadn't been mean, they hadn't had to slam on their brakes, and I would expect that there was no dirty look on their end. We had just had a very polite, very productive honking session. I almost wanted to get out of my car, and run after the person and tell them, "I just honked at another car for the first time!! I didn't hurt your ears did I? No? Good! Have a great night! I'm glad we didn't run into each other!!"

Now, I don't think I'm ever going to start honking like a New York City taxi driver, but honking is cool, I've got to say.

I can't wait to honk again. I wonder, will it take another 10 years, or will it be in three days?

I have no way of knowing, but I can't wait!

So Random
it Hurts So Good

Much of my writing, and for that matter, the things I spend a lot of my time thinking about, are proposed explanations to understand what happens to me or to make sense of the things around me. As I've gotten older (again, a relative term), I've realized that there really is no such thing as a complete understanding of life. It's far too complex, way too unpredictable, and actually way better than can even be explained by reason or cognitive thought.

Case in point: the picture at the top of this page. It's not a large picture, and it may be difficult to see in the small thumbnail. So, I will describe it for you. This is a picture of a white pickup truck in the parking lot at my local dry cleaner. On the inside of the dashboard of this pickup truck sit two windshield sun shades.

These shades are rather popular for motorists who park their vehicles in the sun for long periods of time. They protect the inside of the car's interior from the ruthless heat of the sun and help preserve the condition and color of leather or upholstery on the seats and steering wheel.

The fact that this truck is sporting these shades is not in itself remarkable. What is drop dead amazing is the content of what is on the shades.

Each shade is screenprinted with the words and logo of America Online. And, underneath in blue lettering on each screen is the word Arizona.

What?

What is going on here?

First of all, America Online and Time Warner merged in the year 2000 to form AOL Time Warner. So, that means for these shades to still have a logo the spells out the words America Online that puts their creation date at somewhere before the turn of the millennium.

And the Arizona part of it? I can't find anything on the Internet that suggests AOL was ever regional, or ever did national events where someone would need to represent the state of Arizona. I don't remember any competitions or anything where representatives from each state competed in the AOL Olympics or anything like that.

Why on Earth was an America Online windshield sun shade ever created? What possibly could have been the reason or the occasion?

My mom always told me when I was a little boy, smart kids ask questions. And to this point, I've asked a lot of them.

But I think in some cases, it might be best to let some things go...

Some things are better left just being hilariously random. Better left unexplained. Sometimes what we don't know is actually more fun than if we had.

For all I know this white truck owner could have been a screen printer who had an extra sample of the shades because they still work.

But that's way less interesting than not knowing!

And so for that AOL Arizona, I salute you. I salute the inexplicably hilarious and random, and I salute your owner for keeping you in such fine shape all these years.

I'd really love to see the interior and dashboard of that truck. I bet it looks brand new!

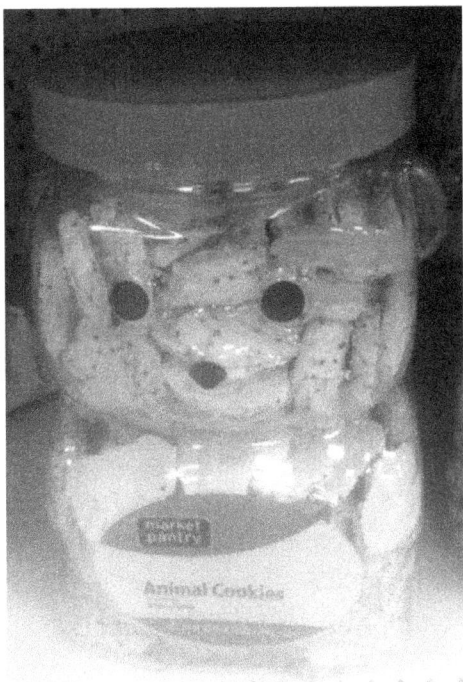

Three Little Black Dots

If it's the little things that make all the difference, then Target should win an award for package design for their frosted animal cookies (I've always called them crackers, and loved that animal crackers were like the only sweet cracker that I knew, but the package clearly states that they are cookies. This is probably the only disappointing thing about this whole package!).

In an age when companies routinely don't go the extra mile if it means they don't make an extra buck, it certainly is nice to see that Target continues to make their plastic canisters in the shape of teddy bears. I'm sure it costs more to make the machine die that molds bear-shaped canisters than simply a cylinder, but I really appreciate their effort.

What value does the bear shape add?

Fun, of course. Target understands that the people eating these cookies are kids. Kids like teddy bears. Teddy bears are awesome in fact. Most adults love teddy bears. And you know what Target wants when people are eating their cookies? Happy customers. Customers who are happily thinking back to their childhood, when they had a teddy bear. Customers who like the canister so much that they save it after the cookies are gone, and store crayons in it. Customers whose children want to come back to Target to get the "Bear Cookies."

Oh yes, Target gets it.

Target gets it so much so that they don't just make the canister a bear shape, they glue three little black paper dots to the inside of the canister that make up the bear's face.

There really is only one suitable word for this: Cute.

If you can look at that bear canister with his eyes and nose and not think that that's cute, you may as well not have a pulse.

I don't just throw around the word "cute" lightly.

To me, seven-week-old puppies are loveable, nice, fuzzy, fluffy, rambunctious, but never cute.

I might stoop to calling an infant precious, or possibly adorable if I'm feeling extra zealous, but even infants are not cute to me.

If a girl asks if an outfit is cute, I will of course say, sure, if that's the case. This implies that I think the outfit is cute, but is not explicit. In my head, I'm thinking one of two things: Yes, I like that outfit; I'd go with a different word, but I know you like "cute," so I'll agree. OR that outfit is way better than cute; cute is not nearly strong enough to describe how I feel about it. Spectacular or above only on that one (For outfits that aren't cute, I don't answer but instead change the subject or just try to smile charmingly. This rarely works.).

The moral of the story is, very few things in life are cute to me. And this bear is in a rarefied class. His contemporaries include little kids' art projects and specifically the way they hold crayons while scribbling.

Old people who still hold the door for each other at restaurants; they are cute.

Fuzzy yellow ducklings are too. We raised those in first grade, and they snuck into my cute filter before I knew what was happening.

I just love this bear canister. Every part of it. The shape. The eyes. The sticker on his belly that looks like it could be a red and white ball just balancing there. Super cute!

The best part of this story: I don't even eat frosted animal crackers!

The Semi-Colon Revival

I don't especially like the semi-colon. I only partially know how to use them, and get nervous most times that I do. I do know that they are used to connect two independent statements, or as a part of a list. But even Wikipedia had to help me put my understanding of the semi-colon into words that other people could understand. While I was browsing old Why-ki, I discovered that semi-colons are also used quite often in academic writing.

Which probably describes why I don't see too many of them. Or, for that matter, why a lot of common people don't see a lot of them—not a lot of common people read academic writing.

I sort of feel pretentious when I use semi-colons. It's almost as if to say, I know how to use a semi-colon; I bet you don't! Although to be fair, I don't always know if I'm using them right, so I'm not sure that counts as pretentious. Or maybe it's an even worse form of pretentiousness, the I-don't-even-know-what-I'm-doing-but-I'm-doing-it-anyway usage. See, I used a semi-colon in this paragraph. Maybe it was used correctly, maybe it wasn't. Do you know?

The sheer fact that humans lived without semi-colons until 1494 is probably enough evidence that the punctuation mark really isn't necessary. Five-hundred years in the lifespan of the written word isn't really that long...So I guess you could say the semi-colon is kind of like the teenager of the punctuation world. Young, misunderstood, cool in some crowds, totally ignored in others. The period is like an overbearing father. When he says something's over, it's over. Period. The comma is like a mother. She has many good traits, but she also can just prolong things, make them go on and on, continuously nag you, repeat herself...You see where I'm headed here. Like the mother, a world without commas leads to total anarchy and complete lack of discipline.

But, a good comma knows when to stop and end the sentence before it becomes an atrocious run on.

The colon is like the cool older brother. He's bold, people always listen when he talks, and he is often followed by groups that will do whatever he commands.

And so that leaves the semi-colon.

Of course there's plenty of others. The attention-starved exclamation point. The clingy apostrophe. (Ted's shoes are actually MY shoes.) The flip-flopping hyphen, and the cross-dressing dash are a pretty delightful combo in their own right.

But what about the semi-colon?

Luckily for her, there has been a momentous movement that's been occurring for a few years now...

Text messaging!

All the sudden the semi-colon is all over the place.

She's like the little sister that was biding her time all along, and then all the sudden, BAM, when did she grow up so fast?

Ladies and gentlemen, we're in the midst of a semi-colon revival.

Who doesn't love to get a text message with a little winky face at the end?

Hey honey, see you tonight ;) The semi-colon is suggestive and seductive...

Hey, good work forgetting to bring the tickets ;) The semi-colon is that friend who knows just how to get under your skin without making you too mad.

Don't worry, I'll never tell mom ;) The semi-colon is mysterious, but also versatile enough to be used correctly, even if you're not sure how it's meant... Are you telling mom, or aren't you? Ugh...

It's pretty ironic that for the world to start using semi-colons —a mark used most often by scholars and academics—it took the condensed format of a text message, and the intellect of flirting 13 year olds winking at each other to bring them back.

I do have to say, I prefer the use of the winking kind of semi-colon. I've never once felt pretentious while using one!

Airline Pilots Must Really Love America

A ir travel is just a boon for people watching and noticing hilarious things, and a recent 21-hour journey to Chicago proved to be no different. Almost from the time you walk into an airport, it's as if there are just buzzers going off everywhere that alert you to the awkward things happening all around you.

There are kids everywhere, crawling on everything, and spitting, drooling and otherwise precipitating in almost every way imaginable. It's hard to imagine a more germ-infested place in the world than the floor of an airport, and there's little Johnny rolling around in street germs and drool. Soon after, his mom hands him a peanut butter sandwich, and you just have to look away because the scene is just too hard to watch.

Then there's the people who bring EVERYTHING with them to the airport. I saw a couple flying from Chicago to Kansas City the other day, and I swear they must have been staying for a month. They EACH had three of the largest suitcases I've ever seen, and a carry-on. Maybe they were moving there? Chicago to Kansas City is only 500 miles away, so if you're going to need to bring half of your house, why not just drive? I don't know, like I say, sometimes you just can't explain what people are doing, but this was unbelievable. Eight bags, two people, Chicago to Kansas City. Mind boggling.

Although, I'm not sure it's as mind boggling as the people who pack their luggage in shall we say, non-traditional luggage. Now, I'm no one to judge people's financial wherewithal to afford luggage, but I once saw a guy checking a cardboard box held together by duct tape and a bungee cord. Luckily, he did put his full address on the box—even if it was the address of the city he was departing from. I am privileged enough to own many duffle bags, suitcases, gym bags, back packs, you name it. Many of them were free promotional items, actually. I feel like a bag is one of the easiest things to just happen into, and to fly with clothes packed in a cardboard box, that just doesn't seem right. I can't imagine the thought process on that one. Well, I guess I'll just pack my clothes in this cardboard box... Chances are if you can afford a plane ticket, you'd think you could afford something more than a cardboard box to transport your clothes...

But by far the best part of the airport experience is the ultra-patriotism displayed by nearly every airline pilot, ever. No matter the airline, no matter the city, no matter the age of the pilot, every one of those dudes LOVES the USA. And it is fantastic.

Big bold bald eagles? You betcha.

Old Glory flapping in the wind? Gloriously, or course.

National monument collages? From Arlington National Cemetery to the White House, baby!

I'd venture to bet that there's not a flat suitcase-toting airman in this great country who doesn't own some sort of red white and blue neck regalia.

Perhaps this stems from a tradition of military men that went on to become pilots in years past. Men that continued to trumpet their pride for their country every time they flew. Or maybe there's a special mix of jet fuel and perfect vision that just makes you want them want to yell, "AMERICA!" every time they get dressed. I'm not sure.

But amidst the lines of snot-dispensing germ hurlers and world's worst pack rats, it sure is nice to see a nice pair of aviators, perhaps a svelte mustache and a necktie that screams, "Don't mess with my country, man!"

I love the USA.

The Somali Cab Driver and the Mongolian Throat Singer

C ab drivers get a bad rap.

Sure, some of them sleep in their cabs, shower monthly and endanger their passengers with every screeching turn they make. Some of them rarely speak, and when they do, it's often in languages we don't understand. Most people think of cab drivers in a similar light as they view telemarketers, used car salesman, or an agent for the TSA.

I have to say, I love cab drivers, and I respect them nearly as much as I do anyone in any profession.

Over the past few months in my travels, I've met cab drivers who were getting MBAs, nursing degrees, and even a future CPA. I met a guy who had worked 20 hours a day seven days a week for six years straight. I met a guy who had been in the United States for 12 years and had never owned a home, an apartment, or any permanent dwelling at all. He had an arrangement with a hotel to get cleaned up in one of their rooms, and he slept in his cab every night waiting out in front of the airport to pick up his first fare. He kept just enough money to live, and sent everything else back to support his family in India.

My most recent cab driver may have been the most impressive of all. He was from Somalia, and he had a passion for culture and history. He spoke five languages, and over the course of our two rides together (I re-hired him after the first ride because I enjoyed his company so much) I had learned more about the Mongolians than I had in my entire life.

I didn't catch the gentleman's name, but I really wish I had.

He started by telling me about his father, and how his father had recently had an operation to remove an esophageal tumor. The process of learning about the procedure had taught himself and his family about the perils of smoking. They had all been smokers, but were brought up not really understanding what was at risk. He said he'd been smoking for years, and as soon as he started to learn about how likely he was to get cancer from smoking, he stopped immediately.

From there, we started talking about the spread of Somalis throughout the United States. I told him I lived in Nashville, and he immediately knew that there was a decent contingent of his native countrymen there, as well as in Memphis. However, it wasn't nearly as heavily populated as Philadelphia, or even Columbus, Ohio. Columbus? Somalia? Interesting.

On our second ride, he really got into his love for learning about history and culture. Before we even started our trek to the airport, we watched a short video, and he read me part of an article on a new theory regarding Mongol warfare.

We talked about the ruthless nature of Genghis Kahn, and the incredibly vast amount of territory that his regime controlled at one time, and their early understanding of antiseptics.

Apparently, to minimize the effects of wounds from sharp-tipped arrows, Mongol warriors wore silk undergarments beneath their armor. The way in which the silk was spun worked in such a way as to tangle around the tip of the arrow, instead of allowing it to just rip right through. The result of this was that in many cases, the silk would form a barrier around the tip of the arrow, and even if the arrow penetrated through the skin of the victim, the layer of silk helped keep out germs and other contaminants from entering the person's body. After removal of the arrow, the affected area tended to be much cleaner, and fewer infections arose as a result.

In some ways, it shouldn't shock me that I was hearing this. Any person has the ability to learn and relay information, no matter if they are a cab driver or a med student.

But I think it's just the way this man has gone about learning what he knows. He told me that any time he's waiting on his next passenger, he's always reading or watching a documentary on his phone. Sometimes only for a few minutes at a time, but over the years, he's been able to learn a lot!

Before I knew it, my next culture lesson was on the techniques of Mongolian throat singing. This is a bizarre technique of singing that seems to involve making sounds that originate from around the Adam's apple area of someone's throat. It's crazy to hear, and while I don't necessarily love it, listening to my driver talk about it was fascinating. He spoke of how it's a dying art, and that there are a dwindling number of throat singers who continue to pass on the technique. He's quite fearful it will die out altogether.

As I was learning all this, there was a part of me that became very sad. American culture frowns on cab drivers, yells at them, disregards them as second-class citizens, and often times goes out of its way to chastise them publicly.

Yet in most cases, the lives of most cab drivers is the modern version of what was the American Dream for most of our ancestors.

Work hard.

Try to assimilate into an existing culture.

Advance socially through education and the willingness to never stop learning.

So many Americans in today's culture are proud of their working-class roots or their inauspicious beginnings. Regularly reveling in the fact that their great-great-grandfather came to this country with nothing but the clothes on his back, worked menial jobs to put food on the table and send his children to school.

And now two hundred years later, there are millions of immigrants doing the same thing, and our culture belittles them for their accents, religious beliefs, or the way they dress.

I sat there in the back of this cab - it was a hybrid, by the way - as my driver was showing me a YouTube video of who was widely believed to be the best living Mongolian Throat Singer, and I got a little tear in my eye. How awesome was this?

I got into a cab just trying to get from Point A to Point B, and I got out knowing this man. Knowing some of his life story. Knowing his passion for history. Knowing more about an ancient culture, and a dying art.

As I got out of the cab at the airport, he took his sunglasses off, looked me square in the eye—the way my parents always taught me to do with someone you respect —and said, "Thank you for the conversation, I really enjoyed it."

I thanked him, too, took my receipt and headed into the airport knowing that I had just had one of the best conversations of my life.

Don't Hire Me to Clean Your House

I am terrible at cleaning. It's one of those things I harp on myself all the time to get better at. To stay up on it, to do it more consistently, and to never let things get out of control. And of course they always do.

It always starts with junk mail. Junk mail makes up about 92 percent of all the mail I get, and yet I still like to look at most of it. I don't look at the super lightweight sale flyers from Clipper Magazine, but pretty much anything that's printed on decent cardstock, I'm a sucker for. Maybe it's the marketing person in me that doesn't want to let down the person on the other end of the mail that created the piece, I don't know.

I come home from the mailbox, and set down my mail, set down my bag from work and usually go about doing something else. Then I'll go work out, or eat dinner, or do some more work on the laptop, and the next thing I know, my house is a mess.

It's like magic. There will be a flyer from the dentist. I'll think, oh yeah, I should go to the dentist. Two weeks later, I throw away the flyer as it's been gathering dust on my counter.

Then I'll start finding mail all over the house. The other day I found a postcard in my spare bedroom / office. It was for a food drive that took place four months earlier. A food drive I didn't participate in, don't remember having any interest in, and can't even remember ever getting the card in the mail in the first place. And yet, there it was!

When I find things like this, especially if it's on a weekend, it drives me crazy. And then I'll just start cleaning. Picking everything up and putting it in drawers, baskets, or any other kind of receptacle.

This usually makes things much worse.

After a pick-up binge, I'll often find things in the strangest spots, or worse I won't be able to find anything at all.

Where did I put my headphones?

Of course it made total sense at the time to put them in the drawer with the kitchen utensils....

For the last year or so, I've stored my extra Ethernet cable with two pairs of scissors... In that case, I just jammed it in the same coffee mug one day, and haven't needed it since...

I also keep DVDs and crayons/sketch books in the same bank of drawers in one of my pieces of furniture. Don't ask me why, but at the time, it helped me "clean" my house.

Putting things away to be orderly—or at least to feign being orderly—is one thing. The day to day cleaning to keep up with bathrooms, the kitchen and the living room are a disaster all their own.

Luckily I live in a small apartment, otherwise, I might have a catastrophe on my hands.

My bedroom always needs picking up, dusting, vacuuming. My sheets always need changing, and I'm about as good at keeping up with my laundry as you are about routinely calling your great uncle...

Bathrooms are the worst though, by far.

I won't repulse you any further—yet—it's just suffice to say it's not pretty. Every weekend, I "plan" to clean my bathrooms, my toilets and my showers, and it never happens. Well, actually it does, but when it does, it's not cleaning, it's like being exercised by a demon.

There's something about cleaning when things are so dirty that just plays with your mind.

To the point where I'm on all fours, in my bathtub with a towel wrapped around my mouth and nose to keep out the fumes from the bleach-based cleaner I'm using to try and cut through the residue of shower buildup I've so graciously been saving for myself. I get to the point where I'm scrubbing so hard with my scrub brush, the burn is akin to a session with a personal trainer. My insanity builds as my eyes widen, eying the mildew on the tile.

Soft plastic shower curtains may as well be the bane of my existence. I swear they laugh at me as I try to scrub them clean. The last time this happened, I actually ended up ripping the curtain down, and ending up in a heap of semi-soggy shower curtain mixed with the smell of bleach. This was not one of those moments you want to end up on camera. My right knee slipped and I ended up on my back, narrowly missing hitting my head on the faucet.

Humiliated, I got out of the shower, only to find that I had washed the floor in the wrong order, and left the floor mat in the other room. So now I had my clean floor, with nothing to stand on, and a dripping wet mixture of dirty shower curtain residue, and the burning of the bleach as it was starting to permeate its way through my skin.

I tried to jump from the bathtub to the carpeted area of my bedroom. That sort of worked, but then in the process, I hit my elbow on the doorframe, causing me to drop the shower curtain on to the clean floor (I had just decided I was going to throw the shower curtain away, since I had ripped it in the process of trying to clean it.).

Dejected, I went outside and put the curtain on my patio, and came into go about finishing cleaning. The rest of the shower wasn't awful, but some of the stains just don't come out, especially in the grout of the tile. So, feeling like less of a human for not being able to keep clean grout, I turned my attention to the rest of the bathroom. Not wanting to make the same mistake of cleaning the floor out of order again, I decided to tackle the toilet.

Again, some details need to be spared here, although I will say it wasn't pretty. At one point, I was sitting on the floor, clutching the side of the toilet bowl, scrubbing up under rim of the toilet, grunting like Serena Williams.

I always used to marvel at my dad when I was little in the way he breathed when he was doing chores. Everything seemed so difficult. Everything made him sweat. I didn't get it.

And yet here I was, sweating on my bathroom floor, trying to get my toilet bowl clean. Breathing heavily, and gritting my teeth.

Who had I become? I was consumed by this task. Possessed to get these dried water marks out from underneath the rim of the toilet.

By the time I finished, I was so exhausted I just laid there with my head propped up against the wall, gasping for air.

Here I was, a grown man, sitting on the floor, straddling a toilet in a 15-sq.-ft.-bathroom. Choking on bleach fumes, with a ring of sweat underneath my backside, I just started laughing.

I was so bad at cleaning, I had made myself laugh.

Then I got up, cleaned the bathroom floor, and walked to Target. It was time to get a new shower curtain.

I stopped at my mailbox on the way home. I threw away every piece of mail, RIGHT AWAY.

I'm So Not Cool Anymore

I'm not exactly sure when it happened, but at some point I became drastically uncool. Maybe not as much so with my peers, but with the younger generation. It's like all the sudden, I turned into a lame old guy—that same lame old guy I've desperately been hoping I'd never become.

I can remember going to the gym in college and seeing guys from the grad schools, and the law programs playing basketball. At the time, these guys were about the same age that I am now, but back then I remember thinking, "Man I hope I never turn into those guys. They're so uncool."

They parted their hair to the side.

They wore shortish, squarish, ill-fitting T-shirts with 10-year-old slogans for things that were never really that cool to start with.

Most of them didn't wear basketball shoes. They wore socks that were always slightly longer than they should have been, and shorts that were just a little too short.

Their legs were really hairy, and they tried so hard that they sweated a lot.

I can remember watching from the other end of the court thinking I'd NEVER be that guy.

***

I play basketball a few nights a week now at an outdoor court at a private high school near where I live. I usually play in the remaining daylight hours after work, and if I'm lucky there are some other guys out there to shoot around with, if not play a game of 3-on-3.

When I first started going over there, the other players looked a lot like kids, and I went through this entire exercise in my brain of trying to figure out how old they were.

I've never been good at judging ages, but finally I saw a kid with a tattoo up around near his collar bone that said "Est. 1994" in Old English script. The kid—actually most of the kids—were heavily inked up, and I started noticing another kid with a '93 on the back of his triceps. And finally, a third kid with an "Alive Since '95" on his forearm. Holy cow! Not only were these dudes heavily into the tattoos, they were all about remembering their birth years, and they were super young in my eyes.

I was wearing a shirt that I had gotten in 2004, and immediately remember thinking, well kid, you were nine years old when I get this shirt; thanks for putting that in ink so I could do the math.

The kid tossed me a basketball and said, "You a runner?"

I was thinking, okay, maybe this kid is smarter than I'm giving him credit for. I was after all wearing running shoes..."Yeah man, I run a little on the trails around here."

The kid looked at me with a perplexed look on his face like I had answered him in Spanish...

Then Est. 1994 piped in and said, "Nahh man, are you runnin with us?"

Ohhhh. Am I a runner? Am I playing in the game that's about to start? When you play in a pickup game, you "run," as in run the court. Then if the game ends, and people want to play again, you "run it back."

I knew that. Duh.

"Oh yeah, sure, I'll run with you guys," I stammered back.

"Well then are you gonna bust it up or what??" '93 was staring at me angrily, waiting for me to do something, but I wasn't quite sure what...

Bust it up. Bust it up. Uhh. I didn't know what that meant.

"Sure thing man, whatever works," I said back, obviously not having any clue what I was talking about.

They all just stared at me, and finally I realized I was holding the ball. They wanted me to shoot the ball.

Bust it up. Start the game? I shot the ball. I made it. Thankfully. '95 caught the ball through the net and threw it to '93. He shot and missed.

'94 was the next to make it, and then he threw the ball to me.

"Alright old man, we ain't losing to these bi***es."

Old man? Oh no, I'm the old man. And we're on a team?

Ahhh. Bust it up was shooting for teams.

I'm really starting to catch on here...

The game was 2-on-2, so from there I figured I'd be pretty good. I'd been playing 2-on-2 for years.

'94 and I passed back and forth, and he hit a shot. "2-36-Pinochle 5" he called out.

The 2-36 I got. We were scoring by 2's and 3's and going up to 36 before the game would end. Pinochle 5 was a mystery to me. But then '93 tossed me back the ball, so I figured maybe that was just some Southern way of saying we were playing make it—take it? Make it—take it being the variation of basketball where if you score, it is your ball again, and the only way the other team can get the ball back is by stopping you from scoring.

Now with the ball in hand, I decided to shoot a three-pointer. I had made my 'bust it' shot, so I was feeling pretty good. And, wouldn't you know it, I made it again. So, now we had a quick 5-0 lead. But then everyone stopped me, and '94 was like, "Dude, it's Pinochle 5."

He handed the ball back to '95, and they took the ball. I was so confused. '95 missed, and then '94 hit a three-pointer for our team.

Okay, did those points count? Am I even playing basketball anymore? I'm so confused.

Now it was our turn again with the ball?

Oh, I see, we got to five points, and it became make it—take it. That's what Pinochle 5 meant...

My goodness, kids these days and their rules.

It seemed to take forever to get to 36, and I was beyond tired.

These kids were running circles around me. I was scraping my way around the court. Fouling guys, elbowing guys for rebounds. Anything to try and contribute. I hadn't scored a point since my three-pointer that didn't count before Pinochle 5, and I was desperate to contribute. '94 was pretty darn good, though, and he was hanging tough with '93 and '95.

Finally with the score 31-28 in favor of our opponents, I banked in about a six-footer off the backboard from the left block. I had gotten a rebound, butted my way into '95, drenched him in sweat, and banked it in hard.

"Bout time, Cube," '94 laughingly said to me as he checked the ball back to '93.

Cube? What was this Cube he was talking about?

I didn't know, but before I knew it, '94 had received the ball back, and hit another three-pointer. We were now up 33-31.

With another three, we'd be at 36, and the game would be "ours." Or at least 5/36th's mine, and the rest his!

Sure enough, '94 rose quickly again and swished in another three to seal it. '95 caught the ball and slammed it down hard to ground. "We lost to one guy, man!" He was not happy.

Smiling ear to ear, '94 came up to me as I was sitting on the bench to side of the court, gasping for air.

"You do work in a cubicle don't you?" he said as he lit a cigarette.

"How could you tell?" I said as I couldn't believe he could smoke at a time like this. I was so out of breath I was sucking in water like I'd been in the desert for a week.

"With socks like that, where else would you work?"

I looked down at my socks. Navy and khaki argyle. Christ. My dress socks from work. No wonder he'd been calling me Cube. Cube was for cubicle.

I then noticed I could see the top of my thighs as I sat on the bench, and it hit me.

My shorts were too short. My shirt was nine years old. I was wearing dress socks, running shoes, and sweating like a wildebeest. I didn't know any of the terminology the kids were using, and I'd just scored five points out of 36. I was dead tired, and drinking out of a water bottle that boasted about its patent-pending system for keeping water cold without ice. I was wearing glasses that were now fogging up as I was breathing heavily, and I had a soreness in my lower back like I had just been sleeping on a park bench for a week.

Oh my gosh. I was old. And super un-cool.

Way more un-cool than the law students from college. They were at least students.

I was nicknamed after a piece of office furniture. The worst kind of office furniture.

'93, '94 and '95 left the court. It was getting dark now. I was already so sore, I could barely move. I really needed to stretch or tomorrow was going to be unbearable.

And then, I realized something. I looked around. Apparently, it had been a few minutes, as the three kids were out of sight now. I didn't care.

I got up on the bench and yelled as loud as I could. "I don't even work in a cubicle!"

It echoed through the valley. I felt so cool!

We'll See You in 49 Years

I n the life of a teenager, there are few things that rival the feeling of getting your driver's license. I can remember like yesterday taking driver's education, getting my driving hours in with my parents, and fretting about taking the driving test. In the life of a fifteen or sixteen year-old, there's really nothing else that matters more than being able to drive.

My birthday was very near the beginning of the school year, so I can recall being one of the first kids in school to get my license, and the envy that followed from younger kids who couldn't yet drive.

I remember just staring at my license thinking, man, I'm so old, I can DRIVE!

I looked at it more closely and the Illinois state seal gleamed back at me. Then I saw something crazy. It said License Expires on 21st Birthday.

My 21st birthday? No way. As a newly-minted sixteen year old, and already feeling old enough to own the world, 21 seems like an eternity away.

Fast forward twelve years or so, and I can't help but think about how long ago sixteen seemed. All the things I've done, all the places I've seen, and all the things I've learned. It's crazy.

What's even crazier, I recently met my first person from Arizona. What's so crazy about that? Nothing really. Just another state in the union. Albeit pretty far from anywhere I've lived in my life. I've vacationed in Arizona numerous times, had some friends live out there very briefly, but never knew a native Arizonan.

Why is this significant?

Well, in meeting my first Arizonan recently at a bar, I stumbled upon a most amazing fact.

A friend of mine is dating a girl from Arizona, and recently we were at a bar where she was asked to present her ID to verify she was old enough to buy a drink. She was, but the server did a double take.

"It's so crazy that your license expires in 2054," the waitress said. "I always get thrown off when people from Arizona come in!"

2054? As in four decades from now? What is going on here?

And sure enough, as I later found out, Arizona driver's licenses expire on the 65th birthday of the person in question.

I couldn't fathom that. How far away is 2054? 2054 was the year in which "Minority Report" was set. Yes, the futuristic sci-fi thriller with Tom Cruise that tries to predict what a life without crime might be like.

The more I thought about it, the crazier it seemed. I couldn't imagine being that kid who got his license at age sixteen, and then looking down to see "License Expires 2054." How must that feel?

"Well, I got my license, and next thing you know, I guess I'll be moving into the old folks home, because I pretty much don't have anything to look forward to until I turn 65..."

My dad started driving in 1969—the same year Neil Armstrong landed on the moon—and by Arizona law, he'd still be driving on his first driver's license!

In fact, an Arizonan born in 1949 could actually still be on their original driver's license today in 2013. That person would have been born during the Truman Administration. Harry Truman!

My Tennessee license has to be renewed three years after I got it, so I'm due in 2015. I see that the TN Department of Revenue has purchased some fancy new IPads where I can go renew my license, but still, I'd rather not. Citizens from the Grand Canyon State are probably laughing at the rest of us as we wait in line while some lady named Beverly tries to see how long she can wait before calling our name.

I could be wrong, but I can't think of any other official document that is valid for such a long period of time. Mortgages typically last no more than thirty years. Treasury bonds the same thing. Magic Johnson once signed a 25-year contract with the

Lakers, and had FDR lived it out all the way, he would have served the longest Presidential term at sixteen years.

But 49 years?

That takes the cake, Arizona. That takes the cake.

If you live in Arizona and are about to get your license, Beverly really shouldn't say "Have a nice day" when you leave the driver's license facility. She should really say, "Have a nice life!"

Are Electrical Outlets in a Perpetual State of Shock?

Y ou'd think by now they'd see it coming!

Marketing—Just for Me!

T o say that I love marketing is an understatement. I will gladly talk marketing campaigns with just about anyone. I love debating the strategic approaches of all of the big brands with anyone who will listen, and I have an opinion on just about any brand—whether I come in contact with that brand or not.

For example, the Dove Campaign for Real Beauty in which Dove tries to get women to celebrate their bodies for exactly what they are, that's genius. Personally, I've never used any of the products that Dove is marketing to those women, but I love what they try to do in the campaign.

When it first came out, I thought Groupon was revolutionary. They used the power of discovering new hot spots as a way to garner interest in new businesses, and businesses got new customers in the process. All the while Groupon built up a huge list of names in which to market to in the future. If there's one thing to know about marketing in the modern era, it would be this: The person with the biggest list of names—and a way to reach those names—wins. It all becomes a numbers game, and in 2013, there's no one better at this game than Amazon. The sheer amount of revenue that Amazon generates off of their email lists is staggering.

Amazon has so many ways to figure out what you like, what you've bought in the past, and what you might need next. If you've ever bought anything from Amazon, you are familiar with the email you'll get two weeks after you've had the product asking you to give your rating in the form of a review. A week after that, you'll get an email that says something like "Here are some other things you might want to go along with that thing you bought a few weeks ago." If you haven't bought anything in a while, Amazon will send you a personalized email with content pulled from the last time you were on their site. If you looked at it a few weeks ago, maybe you're ready to buy it now? Maybe you will, maybe you won't, but Amazon knows that there's a chance. And, they also know that less than 0.01% of people will unsubscribe from their email list based on a single email. Translation: There's almost no risk to send you an email. Maybe they'll make some money off of you today, maybe next month. Maybe next year, but they will get you!

Amazon is so good at this it's almost silly.

And then, every once in a while, they screw up.

Today I got an offer for a personalized deal "Just For Me."

This came from Amazon Local, a competitor to Groupon, and something I almost NEVER click on.

The offers from Amazon Local are usually pretty decent. Some sort of city tour (I live 15 minutes from a city that I don't know very well that has tons of attractions, so this is pretty sensical), cheap food at a local restaurant (pretty much a safe bet for any twentysomething near a big city), or some sort of "once a year" type activity (zip-lining, skydiving and helicopter tours are popular group events that are easy to do once, and great to do in a group—these show up a lot).

But today, I've got to say, Amazon missed.

Today, they invited me to a Mystery Dinner | Acupuncture. And of course they reminded me that these deals were just for me.

Just for me, huh Amazon?

I immediately started racking my brain for any time in the past two decades where acupuncture had ever crossed my mind. Blank. None. I'm honestly not sure I've ever even considered acupuncture in my life. I'm pretty sure that's where they poke you with little sticks and it's supposed to make you feel better, right? Maybe if I clicked into the email I'd find that this deal was with a world-renowned acupuncturist, and that immediately they'd melt every last ounce of stress from my body.

But I was still too dumbfounded to click. So I reread the subject line of the email again, and realized there was a Mystery Dinner attached to this offer that I hadn't even considered yet.

A Mystery Dinner!

Now this had me somewhat intrigued as well. Where did they hold this mystery dinner? Was there a set, or a place that specializes in mystery dinners? Do they do multiple shows, or is it always the same one?

Is it like Clue? Do you have to go around looking for Colonel Mustard? Does the table have candlesticks? It has to, right? Does it matter that I'm terrible at Clue and am like 0-39 in my career playing it?

Despite all these questions, I'm still not sure how I feel about mystery dinners. I mean, maybe the mystery is what you eat, and it's just a place that doesn't let you actually order food, you just have to eat whatever it is that they give you. That could be the real mystery of it all. What is that meat we're eating? I don't know!

Or maybe it is like a dress up adventure mystery party.

That sounds kind of cool, but I'm not sure how I feel about that going on during a dinner.

I'm still not too adventurous when it comes to dinner. I'm in my late twenties, and I still get chicken tenders a lot. So, I'm not totally positive I could even handle the adventure.

And then, I had an even crazier thought: What if the Mystery Dinner and the acupuncture were together?

Since I received the email, I did some research and actually found out that this character | is called the vertical bar. The vertical bar actually is used in some cases in math to denote division. So, in all truth, in strict mathematical terms, Amazon was separating the two activities.

But my racing mind didn't know that at the time!

A mystery dinner with acupuncture?

Can you even imagine that?

I'm pretty sure they'd probably just serve shish kabobs. You finish eating, and your neighbor could just start poking you with your empty skewers. In fact, there's nothing that even says you would have to be done with your food. As long as you had the meat on there securely, your neighbor could puncture away long before you had finished eating (Author's note: In this case I probably wouldn't suggest overcooking the veggies. Overcooked veggies on a kabob are prone to falling off the skewer. Zucchini and squash can be hard little buggers to keep control of if they get mushy. And the last thing you want is a squash in your shoulders. A good kabob is usually soaked in some lemon pepper, and I'm not really sure how good that is for the skin...).

Maybe Amazon is on to something here. The restaurant could offer a multiple course meal with instructors on site. By the end of the night, the entire party could be halfway to their ABMA (American Board of Medical Acupuncture) Certification. I could really see this working...

I'm not sure how people would feel about having to eat without clothes, but hey, those are just details, right? I mean, if they give you 50% off AND the possibility to get a board certification, you pretty much have to eat naked, right?

So finally, I opened the email. Ready for adventure. Looking for a great deal!

And what do I find?

THIS DEAL IS ONLY FOR THE WESTERN SUBURBS OF CHICAGO?

Amazon, the great and mighty marketing Goliath that they are doesn't know that I moved from the western suburbs a year and a half ago? I'm an Amazon Prime member, I've shipped to five different addresses within the state of Tennessee since the last time I had anything sent to Illinois, and they can't figure out how to send me deals for Nashville?

Who is this company?

Here I was, ready to eat dinner in the nude while complete strangers jab me with shish kabob skewers and drip lemon pepper on my shoulders, and this is how they repay me?

What a bunch of amateurs...

Really Bad Snacks

I t's pretty well documented that there are a lot of overweight Americans. As a whole, we don't exercise enough, we eat too much, and we drink too much—and we pay the price.

Truthfully, I blame food photographers. They are just far too good at their jobs. A talented food photographer can make a steak from Golden Corral look good on a commercial. And that's hard to do!

They can make steak sizzle, chicken wings chant and actually make French fries look slimming.

Food scientists don't help our cause either. They can make any food taste like any other food you can think of. As if I needed bacon-flavored sausage, or key lime cream cheese. Just when you thought you've willed yourself away from eating a food, those darn food scientists go and ad a flavor to it that you can't possibly say no to. Would you like a bratwurst with cheddar, bacon and three servings of masculinity? Well, if you put it that way, give me two....

Burger King will serve you a Whopper for breakfast, you can buy about 3,000 calories for five bucks at Taco Bell, and White Castle will actually allow you to order sliders online with special pricing between midnight and six a.m.

In case you couldn't get enough pizza, you can be sure to remind yourself that you can get it deep dish, by the pie, by the slice, wrapped up as a calzone, as a puff, a bagel bite, a pizza roll and my personal favorite, pizza on a burger. Yes, the glorious minds at the Boston's Sports Bar chain have actually devised a way to put pizza on a hamburger.

It's no wonder Americans snack so much. If we didn't, we might eat six meals a day.

It's no surprise we lead the world in obesity year in and year out.

What is utterly shocking is when you come across a terribly bad snack. After all, our brightest minds can't figure out how to devise an engine that gets 200 miles per gallon or how to grow a strand of corn that grows without water. No, our best minds are trying to figure out how to make fat-free yogurt taste like the richest French silk pie you've ever had. And they are succeeding!

It's one thing to come across a bad snack that's supposed to be bad. Well, no snacks are really supposed to be bad, but there are some that are expectedly bad.

Salt-free pretzels? How did those ever sound like a good idea?

Fat-free garlic and herb rye crisps? I think I'd rather eat rabbit food...

But I'll give these things a pass. Health food disguised as snack food isn't really snack food after all.

It's hard to make a bad snack that's also bad for you, because let's face it, the worse it is for you, the better it tastes.

Although the fine people at the Lays potato chip company have done it. With help from us, America!

A while back, Lays announced the winners of their Do Us a Flavor Contest. They asked America to go on Facebook and nominate their best new flavor ideas, and the ideas with the most support would be made into special edition Lays.

America chose three finalists, with the winner promised a million dollars!

Now I didn't have all three flavors, and I've heard good things about Cheesy Garlic Bread and Sriracha, but that's not what this essay is about.

This story is about Lays Chicken and Waffles Flavored Potato Chips. Which are, quite possibly America's worst snack food. Chicken and waffles are of course a totally American creation. Let's take some good wholesome fried chicken, load up the rest of the plate with some big fluffy waffles, maybe a few generous pads of butter, and then let's just drown the entire concoction in about a third of gallon of syrup. And then, let's call that breakfast.

Lays seemed to realize that there really wasn't anything that could be more American than that, and they captured it in another American favorite: the potato chip.

Except they didn't. They failed so miserably, I think I'd rather drink TAB.

I had a group of friends coming to visit me in Nashville at the beginning of April. As a formal welcome to the South, I figured what better thing to buy than a fresh bag of Chicken and Waffles chips? No sooner had everyone showed up when I proudly busted out the shiny new blue bag. I passed them around with a huge smile on my face...

And nothing.

Less than nothing.

My friends ate, and it was as if momentarily their emotions stopped working. Finally, I had a chip.

Temporary paralysis set in.

What was I tasting?

There was a hint of syrup. I think. And then the next thing I remember tasting was the granularity of the seasoning itself. I think I briefly tasted something that might have supposed to have been chicken, but it really just made my tongue tingle in a strange way. I looked around and my friends seemed to be equally as confused.

"Dude, these aren't good," my friend Andrew said wryly. Andrew likes mostly anything, and for him to speak up in such a manner was as incriminating as it was surprising. The rest of the way around the table, everyone looked the same way, and agreed, we were in the presence of mediocrity.

We each ate about four chips, and the results did not improve. My friend Shana ate a few more, as did I. About three chips later, we looked at each other, and in unison, we both said, "Why are we still eating these things?"

For the rest of the visit, I kept the chips out of the cupboard, just in case anyone wanted to munch away. No one did.

My friends eventually left. I tried to pawn the chips off on them as well. They didn't bite. So, I sheepishly put the three-quarters-full bag back in the back of the cupboard. I felt silly. Here I had tried to do something cool for my friends, and it had failed. They didn't care, and I knew it wasn't a big deal, but secretly I had really hoped they were a hit.

I put them back in the cupboard because I have a tough time throwing food away. I didn't know how long they'd sit there, but I just didn't want to throw them away.

Six months later, they're still there.

I've been in the cupboard approximately 921 times since then, and never once have I had even the slightest urge to open that bag. I see it every time, and immediately my mouth dries up. The top of my throat gets dry, and any ounce of appetite momentarily leaves me (Think Lima beans—they are the only other food that has the effect on me.).

I challenge any of you to a six-month Bad Snack Challenge. Go to the store, buy a non-healthy snack that you've never had before. And, don't just buy chocolate-covered orange slices if you don't like oranges. Buy something you think you might like.

From there, I challenge you to eat one serving of the snack and then not touch it again. For 180 days. Or, 78 reasonless cravings, 19 sleepless nights, the eight times you're completely out of food, and the one time every six months you even think of lima beans...Try not to eat that snack.

If you can accomplish this feat, I will put your snack on this dubious pedestal. Until then, Lays Chicken and Waffles Potato Chips will hold the title of America's worst snack. And man, do they deserve it!

I Still Love Good Charlotte

I was in high school during a pretty terrible era for music. Most specifically, pop-punk-emo music was pretty popular at the time, and being the impressionable lemming that I was, I was all about it. I actually remember claiming to 'Love Good Charlotte!" If you know of Good Charlotte, I hope you can snicker at this statement for a few minutes at my expense. If you don't, thank you for not contributing to the slow destruction of our society by supporting their music (They didn't like their dads, and they proved EVERYONE wrong when then "Made It.").

There have been some pretty awesome eras to grow up in music-wise – the late Sixties, the legendary classic rock days, the big hair band Eighties days—even the early Nineties grunge scene was pretty formidable in comparison to my coming of age years. Twenty years from now, I really don't think history will look back too fondly on the early to mid-2000's popular music scene. The "Post Boy Band Nickelback, 50 Cent, Britney Spears, Trainwreck Years" probably won't have the same influence that AC/DC, Led Zeppelin and Pink Floyd had...

Today I listened to the same Good Charlotte album I had in my car CD player for about seven years from 2002 to 2009. And I cringed. I cringed badly. How did I like this stuff? The album was aptly titled "The Young and the Hopeless." That's a laughter inducer right there. The lyrics to the songs were so bad, I couldn't help but laugh. But there was an important thing that came out of this exercise, and it was very positive (You didn't think I was just going to rail on Good Charlotte for an entire essay did you?).

Music is such a powerful trigger of emotion and memory. It's phenomenal. I hadn't heard Good Charlotte for at least five years, and during that time, I was trying my hardest to listen to anything and everything that was better than their music, and at the same time listen to as many songs as possible just to forget they existed. And yet, as soon as I heard the first song on their Hopeless album, it was like instant time travel.

I was back in Illinois in 2002. I was in my old car. I was driving to play Frisbee golf. I can see my old Nokia 'Brick" cellphone sitting in the cup holder. I can even remember a dark blue T-shirt and cargo short combo I wore on a certain day. It's raining. I'm speeding. And I'm full of angst over whether or not the Frisbee golf course is going to be too wet to play. My CD player operated on a little remote that was connected through my car radio, and I can remember flipping through the songs on that album and pounding the steering wheel in the out of rhythm cadence that is my dubious signature for most things in life...I can remember it like yesterday.

Today, I was walking past the front of a store that had a speaker on the outside amplifying sound for all to hear. Out rang the familiar sound of Jimmy Eat World's "The Middle." I immediately thought, "What year is this, 2002?"

No sooner had I thought it, the radio DJ proclaimed that had just been Jimmy Eat World with the No. 14 song on their countdown of the top 15 songs of 2002. I found myself transported back to the baseball field at Naperville Central High School where I had put that same song on a warm-up mix for the Redhawk baseball team. I actually began to taste sunflower seeds in my mouth back in 2013. Barbecue flavor, the kind I was obsessed with in 2002. I couldn't believe it.

I know I'm not the only one to realize this connection. People have been hearing their First Dance Wedding Songs for generations and reliving their magical nights every time they do. Many people remember what songs were playing on the radio when they were driving to the hospital to give birth to a child, or driving across country on a road trip in their childhood.

Every time I hear Bob Seger, I'm transported back to a Chevy Astro van, driving with my dad to go to the hardware store. He's wearing a red flannel shirt. I'm about four years old, and I'm sure Pops is laughing in his head as I ask him if he thinks Bob Seger actually likes rocks.

I'm sure Bob Seger likes rocks in his own special way...
In that same special way that I still love Good Charlotte.

Why Does Columbus Impel People to Buy Cheap Mattresses?

I love ads, and I love advertising. For the most part, I think it's ingenious to make up a sale or promotional event. In fact, it's my job to get people to care about products and services, so if a silly sale or promotion is going to help that process, I'm all for it.

But why does Christopher Columbus get his own weekend devoted to selling cheap furniture and electronics?

I don't watch a lot of live TV, so luckily I'm spared from a lot of the ultra-obnoxious announcements that remind me that THIS WEEKEND ONLY!!!! I can get a brand new, premium queen size mattress set for ONLY THREE HUNDRED AND NINETY NINE DOLLARS! But man, even hearing it once is enough to make my brain hurt.

I know there are a lot of made up sales conveniently positioned around holidays, but this one always gets me.

Black Friday is, of course, ridiculous, but I get it. People are off work, it's near Christmas, retailers need to get people in their stores to buy up old inventory before the year ends…

Memorial Day and Labor Day, people are again off work, and a good sale is a good reason to get them into a store on their day off. Plus, Memorial Day is the unofficial start of summer, so it's a good time to stock up on summer essentials and new lawn furniture, of course! Labor Day closes out the summer, and is the perfect time to start thinking about fall items.

Even President's Day I sort of get. Combine Lincoln and Washington's birthdays, fly out some American flags and put carpet on sale. It's February, after all, what else is there to do? It's snowy and dreary in the North, and football's over in the South, so that pretty much seals it. Technically you can hunt small game until February 28 in many states, but after a four-month hunting season, you can only kill so many quail before buying carpet even seems like a decent idea...

Columbus Day sales make no sense, though. Is October really that different from Labor Day? It's still not summer and going into fall. Buyers' needs really haven't changed. The colors are changing, and as the weather gets cool, people need to buy new clothes, but that hardly warrants a sale. Just put new sweaters on display in warm orange, yellow and brown shades; you don't need Christopher Columbus to get women into your store. A couple of cinnamon-scented Yankee Candles and complimentary pumpkin spice lattes, and you could probably sell those sweaters at 20 percent over list price...

And what does Columbus have to do with mattresses? In his time, the dude slept on mattresses that were made of pea shucks. Pea shucks! Also, I have issue with Columbus anyway. Once you get passed sailing the ocean blue in 1492, you come to realize that he wasn't really that good of a guy. His treatment of Native Americans is legendarily bad, and the further you look into him, the worse it gets. Plus, it's not like America has this long-standing tradition of upholding our relationship with the fifteenth century Spanish. Queen Isabel Day? I don't think so.

I mean, there is Mayflower Moving Company. I guess that's a decent thing that came out of the whole deal. Better than cultural displacement, and the widespread introduction of infectious disease, at least. Oh wait, I'm mixing my stories with the Pilgrims at Plymouth Rock... Ugh...

If anything should be on sale during Columbus Day, it should be flu shots. Save up to 14.92% on a disease fighter than Columbus himself would be proud to know he helped make necessary!

I honestly think that American retailers would have more luck selling merchandise if they all got together and decided to make up a sales holiday based around Oprah, Ronald Reagan and Chuck Norris.

This weekend, buy everything that Oprah says, and we'll give you 15 percent off. The deals are so good, even Chuck Norris takes advantage of them. And, you know it's a good idea, because Ronald Reagan would have supported this idea if he were still around today...

While you're at it, I'm sure Oprah has good recommendations for box springs, sheets with a good thread count, and a dashing duvet cover.

But, you better buy now, because deals this good won't come around for like six whole weeks—when they are better.

Long live Columbus and my mattress. I'll be sure to own it for the next 30 years. That'll show 'em!

Oh No, I Missed One!

I 'd like to think I'm decent enough at personal hygiene not to be offensive. I shower most days, and I get great joy out of brushing my teeth. One time, I accidentally used conditioner instead of shampoo for a month before I realized the "shampoo" didn't seem to lather much. But in general, I do alright. And for that month, my hair might not have been that clean, but it sure was soft!

If there is one area of personal care that I could use some work on, it's shaving. First off, it's really just not that fun to do. My hair is coarse, and unless my beard has grown in a bit, the shaving process is full of a lot of uncomfortable tugging and pulling. And yes, I use Gillette's most advanced anti-tug-and-pull razor you can buy: The Fusion Turbo Power Glide Phantom Midnight Can We Possibly Add One More Name to This Razor Razor.

Whether it's Barbasol shaving cream, Edge Pro Gel, hand soap, shampoo suds, nothing seems to make the process any better. I remember turning eighteen, and Gillette mailed me a razor as like a "Welcome to Manhood" birthday present. They wanted me as a lifelong customer, and I was just happy to get some cool free swag in the mail. It tells you a little something about how cool 18-year-old me was to think that a razor was "cool free swag" but hey!

I remember the first time I was shaving, I filled up the bathroom sink with water and was in the process of hacking into myself against the grain of my skin and my dad came by and just kind of laughed and asked, "Do you even know what you're doing?"

I made some wisecrack about how he couldn't grow facial hair to save his life, and he just kept on walking. In his head, I'm sure he said, "Okay kid, do it your way."

Eventually, I think we did have some sort of shaving lesson, but it must not have been that good. To this day, I get by. Most of the world probably doesn't know the anxiety I feel every time I shave, or the fact that my disdain for the activity often times just results in the three, four, five and eight day stubbles.

Although, there is a great sense of relief that comes from having just shaved. Primarily, it means that I won't have to do it again for a few days—er week—if I can avoid formal meetings or client get-togethers. It is also—despite the lengths I have to go to get there—my state of grooming that is most preferable. It's nice to have a freshly shaved face that feels smooth and clean.

It's nice to walk outside and feel clean air rush into your pores, and even feel a little bite of the cold in the winter. It wakes you up. It gets your blood flowing.

There is, however, one quite terrible revelation in this process. The revelation that you missed a spot during the shaving process. For me, this happens nearly every time I shave, and after it does, the paranoia rivals that of wondering whether or not that bunch of leaves your ran into in the forest was poison ivy or not? Will people notice? How dark is the hair that I missed?

You see, the problem first makes itself known when you run your hand over your face to gauge how well you've done on this most recent job (Author's Note: I realize that this process should take place before I leave the house, and not after, but what can I say, I'm not perfect). Usually, the mid-cheek area is pretty clean. This area is relatively smooth and easy to shave. The chin is also usually pretty clear. It's right in front of your face when you're shaving, so it's pretty hard to leave something glaring there. The trouble areas for me are always underneath the bottom corners of my jawbones, kind of where the neck, jaw and ears all come together. You could say it's like the Bermuda Triangle for razors. The angle is weird, it's hard to see over there, the jawbone sticks out funny so you can't put the razor in the same position as you're used to on any other side of the face. It's really tough. After you notice that you've missed some hairs in this area, total panic sets in.

First, you feel the rogue hairs during one of your sweeps past the jawbones, and this pitting feeling comes to your stomach.

After a few more disbelieving pets, the patch of hair may as well be the size of a three-acre backyard. Four hairs can feel like a football field on the corner of your face. Then, instinctively, you try to contort your skin to prove to your brain that what you just felt wasn't actually there and was a mental illusion. This rarely works.

From there, my experience tells me it's best to then go into full-out cover up mode with any potential human interactees. I mean, for all intents and purposes, you've got a rhinoceros horn sticking out of your jaw area, you can't let that be seen! Walking by someone is pretty easy; you just swipe the hand casually down the face as you pass them. A slight twinge of discomfort on your face can easily sell the fact that may you have a toothache or that one of those annoying little bugs just landed on you.

Sitting in a work meeting is a much tougher predicament. Gathering around a table to brainstorm, or to work on an in-depth project spells multiple hours of close-range facial exposure to potentially very discriminating eyes. On post-shave days, I often pull out the collared sweater/pullover complete with company logo. This not only shows tremendous company spirit around the office, it also provides a high collar to slink the side of my face into to hide my rhino horn.

On warmer days, I just have to be content with the fact that I'm probably going to have to assume expressions of deep thought nearly constantly. Without a top layer cover up and unwilling to stoop to the level of popping my shirt collar, it's a lot like going out in the middle of a driving range with a fly swatter. You can think as deeply as you want, scratch a million phantom itches, and otherwise divert attention as much as you want. Eventually someone will nail you.

For the most part, people are polite. I haven't had anyone give me too much grief for my unintentional jawbone grazing pastures. I've seen people definitely notice, chuckle to themselves, and continue on. But I'm sure I got beet red during these occasions.

YES, I know I'm not good at shaving, but it's not like you have to go tell the whole world I'm a bed wetter! This is way overdramatic, I know.

Some days, there's just nothing you can do about it. You just have to be the farmer that forgot to plow under that one row of corn, and you have to march on with pride.

Luckily, I've gotten smarter recently. I've started to carry extra disposable razors in my car. On numerous occasions, I've had to bail myself out with a last second touch up before heading into a building. It almost feels like bringing a calculator to a math test, but this is one case where I am actually okay with cheating the system. I've been feeling much better since I've employed this system. I've been rogue hair free since August of 1-3. It has a nice ring to it doesn't it!

Although, do me a favor the next time you see me. Don't look too close. I didn't even get into nicks and blemishes...

What Those Hands Have Seen...

I saw an old man washing his hands today underneath an auto-matic faucet. You know, the kind where you just hold your hand underneath and pretty soon the water comes out. He did it with ease. Not that it's a difficult task, but the mannerisms with which he moved his hands, and the liver spots on them placed his age somewhere in the 83-85 year-old range, and not all people this age catch on as quickly to things of this nature. He moved slowly as he put the foaming soap on his hands and washed thoroughly. He then waved at the automatic paper towel dispenser, approximately six inches of brown paper came out, he dried his hands and went on his way. The man wore a sport coat and jeans, even though he was almost certainly retired. His hair was white, and he walked with a slight limp. He didn't look overly wealthy, but at the same time, he also didn't look disheveled.

Before he put his hands into his pockets as he walked out of the bathroom, I thought to myself, "Wow, of all the things those hands have done, I bet that man never thought he'd leave a bathroom without ever touching anything, and wash his hands in the process."

This man most likely was born around 1930 or so. His family survived the Great Depression, and he grew up as a young teenager most likely looking up to the servicemen fighting and coming home from World War II. Based on his limp, he may have served in Korea, and most likely made a name for himself in his profession in the late Fifties and Sixties. Man, what a last 50 years it must have been for him! To see that nation's attitudes change during the Vietnam War, the Cold War, and the War on Terror. To see our country go from a manufacturing boom after World War

II to outsourcing everything and now to trying to bring it all back again to support our own workforce.

What does a man like this see when he sees nine year-olds on smart phones complaining to their mothers that Candy Crush isn't fair? What does he see when a generation of our nation's youth learn morals from Grand Theft Auto, and look up to Lil' Wayne and Miley Cyrus as role models?

One could argue that every generation has always thought the next generation was the next sign of the apocalypse, and you could even argue that idolizing war heroes isn't actually that much better than shooting up virtual cars...

But here's where I think the difference is: Do people of the most current generation have any appreciation for the past? I don't know. I'm sure some do. A lot don't. It seems like people have lost perspective. Many kids these days would probably see that 80-plus-year-old man in the bathroom and never think twice. Never realize that for 80-plus, he's doing alright with all these newfangled contraptions. The man may have had a party line telephone growing up, now every nine year-old can do more with his phone than you could do on the first supercomputer.

As a society, how do you instill that sense of appreciation into the attention deficit generation?

People need to see those hands. Need to see those liver spots, and see the work, the hardship, the pain, and the triumph.

After all, an 80-plus-year-old man just showed those automatic bathroom implements who's really the man! Here's to you old man, here's to you!

The Human Order of Operations

H umans are most certainly creatures of habit. I'm pretty sure
if we filmed ourselves going through our routines each day,
they are pretty similar. Mine goes something like:
Wake up
Turn off alarm
Look out window for four minutes
Doze off for one minute
Turn off alarm again
Get out of bed
Go to the bathroom
Shower...
It's amazing how if the alarm doesn't Go off, or you wake up
thirty minutes before the alarm, it's like someone pulled the rug
out from under you. Or, if your alarm usually goes off at 6 AM, and
for some reason one day you have to set it to wake up at 5:45,
that extra fifteen minutes may as well be an hour...
Dry off
Get dressed
Find an undershirt
...If you go to put on an undershirt and no undershirts are clean
there's a sense of panic that seems to set in. Even if you have
another shirt that you can wear as an undershirt, if it's not
specifically an undershirt, and the collar feels funny, or it has a
graphic that shows through the light colored top layer you're
wearing, it's very uncomfortable...
Find a pair of pants
Match a belt with the pants
Match shoes with belt and pants

Find some shirt that doesn't look horrible with the rest of all that

Make bed

Sit on bed and put socks and shoes on

...This step, if done out of order, is ridiculous. I am a left sock, right sock, left shoe, right shoe kind of guy. Maybe this has to do with being left-handed? I don't know. But if I try to put the right sock on first, my brain can't handle it. And get this, the other day, I put on my left sock first, everything was fine and dandy, and then it was like an alien possessed my body and I put my left shoe on immediately. I sat there paralyzed for like thirty seconds. I had my left sock AND shoe on, and my right foot was completely bare. I stared at my right foot for a while, and it started to look funny. I began to wonder if my ankle bone always stood out that much. And then my left foot started to sweat. It was like it couldn't handle the uneven heating that was resulting from this situation...

Clean up hair – comb, style, or something (I'm not sure what you call what I do)

Brush teeth

Turn off bedroom lights

Find keys

Grab computer bag

Grab breakfast to go

Take multi-vitamin

Leave for the day

Lock door

Pat down packets checking for phone, wallet, etc.

Check email on way to car

Get in car

Check car for work access badge...

Drive to work.

And that's just the morning!

Nearly every morning starts just like this. Your routine might be slightly different. For many, it probably includes coffee, or TV, or reading the paper, or checking the weather, putting on makeup, etc., but chances are it's pretty similar. It probably takes you somewhere between 30 and 90 minutes, and on most days you probably complete your list of tasks within a 2-3 minute window. My routine from start to finish takes 28 minutes. There's pretty much no two ways about it. I know immediately in the shower if I'm running late and try to make up for it, but if I'm not out of the shower by sixteen minutes into the process, I'm toast. I must be in the car and driving by 28 after the hour, or I can't make it to work by the top of the hour.

It's amazing that our bodies work like this.

I did a social experiment on myself. I set one of the clocks in my room four hours and seven minutes faster than the actual time (407 being Duke Snider's—my favorite Brooklyn Dodger—career home run total). Some mornings I woke up facing one way, and don't look at that clock. Other mornings, I did woke up that way and the first thing I saw was that clock. Upon seeing that clock, and having the time be 10:07, my mind flew into overdrive for a split second. Thinking I had slept through a conference call, or was late for a meeting, I'd spring out of bed, flustered and in an instant panic. This only happened twice in five days before my mind remembered that the clock was wrong and to subtract 4:07 from its time, but those two days were rough. It was like I got off to a bad start from the instant I woke up, and I was slightly off the rest of the day. On both of those days I missed my 28-minute deadline for getting ready and actually was later getting to where I needed to be than usual. It was as if my flustered state of mind didn't allow me to concentrate, and even though I was moving faster, I wasn't able to complete my normal tasks as well as usual. I remember being irritable those days, and laughing out loud at the old statement, "Well, didn't you wake up on the wrong side of the bed today?" In fact, I had. Or at least looking off of the wrong side of the bed.

In math, there are rules for the order for which you must do things. You might remember "Please Excuse My Dear Aunt Sally" from grade school. Parentheses, Exponents, Multiplication, Division, Addition and Subtraction must be done in that order within a problem to get a correct answer. Sometimes teachers teach this using the mnemonic device, PEDMAS.

Similarly, my mornings must go like, WTLDLGGSDGFFMMFMS-

CBTFGGTLLPCGCD, or things just don't work out. It's what I like to call the human order of operations, and boy is it tricky!

Anyone that can come up with a mnemonic device to remember that one, I'll shake your hand!

Engineered to Perfection

I've still got a lot of living left to do. A lot I still want to learn. A lot I still want to share. I'm hopeful that my blessings have only just begun.

But in one respect, I've already reached one of the most important summits in my life: I have experienced the pinnacle of shower head operational design.

What follows is what is undoubtedly a First World rant. I understand that in many parts of the world, they'd kill for running water let alone a clean shower. Nonetheless...

There are very few things in the world that I will flat out rip on, but a bad shower is one of them. First of all, who wants to stand in a shower where the water piddles out of the showerhead like it's an 80-year-old prostate? If you're at the point where you can stand under the shower head and the water hits your head, and doesn't make it all the way through your hair to your scalp, you should just get out immediately. You'd be better off putting your head under the sink and spraying your body with a garden hose.

And what about those showers where the shower head is mounted on the wall about three and a half feet from the floor. The water comes out and hits you in awkwardly in between the neck and the collar bone. It hits your Adam's apple area, and if the water pressure is at piddle it almost feels like someone is trying to drape a wet scarf around your neck. It's the worst.

And then to top it all off, trying to figure out how to change the temperature in the shower should not require a doctorate. Is it to the right or the left for hot water? Or is it which way the base of the handle points? Because those are complete opposites...And if the handle rotates a continuous 360 degrees, just forget it, you can go from scalding to frozen with one over-zealous turn of a slipper handle. And to think, all of this could be happening when an angry midget is trying to climb on your neck and attack you with a limp, damp scarf of water.

The only thing that can actually make this worse is if you're in one of those hotel showers with the built in anti-slip mats that help make sure the elderly don't fall down. They're always too soft and squishy. It feels like you're walking on a floor that is entirely made of the material of moldy old shower sandals. Again, by this time, showering in the sink usually seems like a better option.

Throw in less than ample shelf space for shampoo, or bar soap, and no hanging apparatus for wash clothes, and you may be better off showering in jail. Okay, maybe that's a little extreme, but does it really have to be that hard to design a great shower?

In fact, I have the best shower of all time at home.

It's water pressure is perfect. A few PSI less than painful, but powerful enough to wake you up in the morning.

The operation is intuitive and repeatable. One part of the dial operates water pressure: all the way on for full pressure, and less as you get closer to the water being off. Easy enough, right? The temperature control is another lever that is completely disconnected with water pressure. So, you can actually adjust the temperature with the water off if you'd like—or wait until it's on, whatever works for you. Hot is to the left, just like at a sink, and cold is to the right. There is no turning this lever 360 degrees to get confused about which is hot or cold, or if the top or the bottom of the lever is the indicator for the temp. It's always pointing up, and whichever way you turn it, corresponds with what you think it would. The greatest part of this feature is that you can leave the temperature at your desired level at all times, and just turn the water on and off. No looking for your desired temp. If you want, you can leave it at the same spot day after day. I don't know about you, but I don't like to be doing any guess work in the shower in the A.M.!

My shower has a good sized shelf for bar soap, and plenty of ledge space for bottles of hair cleansing product. In addition, the shower head is at a height than can accommodate a normal-sized human and actually wash their hair. There's even a hanging bar in the back to hand a wash cloth, or attach a shower caddy.

I'm telling you. Perfection.

I wish I could just invite every hotel chain operations person to my house and give them a demo of this engineering marvel.

Actually, I'd like to take it a step further. On Hotels.com, Kayak, Priceline, all of those sites, I'd like to make shower rating a filterable variable when I book a room. I don't care if it's the best room in the Ritz Carlton, if the shower is a dud, the room is going to be less than stellar. A five-star room can turn into a three-star mistake with a bad shower.

I don't need a heated floor, or a ledge to sit on when I shower. I don't need a fog resistant mirror, or an adapter for my iPod. All I really want is a shower that's easy to operate that dispenses water at a reasonable pressure rate.

I guess I'll just have to live in my current apartment forever. Once you've seen perfection, it's impossible to go back!

OfficeMax Should Sell Sportcoats

Office supply stores have been coming up with unique and ingenious ways for people to store important documents for years. The folder is a good one, so is the envelope. The briefcase had a pretty good run, as has the fancy leather bound portfolio. While I'm at it, I'd love to pay credence to the clear plastic sleeve, the three-ring binder, the long cylindrical mailing tube, and it's more distinguished cousin that transports fancy old maps.

The spiral bound notebook, hanging file, Rolodex, and Banker's Box may be on their way out in this era of digitized storage via the memory card, flash drive, and who can forget the cloud. Most of my life is in the cloud, and while I applaud its efficiency, ease of access, and relative lack of an environmental footprint, there's something the cloud does not evoke.

Emotion.

That feeling I get when I thumb through my mom's accordion-style recipe folder and find an old recipe printed on a water-melon-themed recipe card. The sense of nostalgia I get looking through old photo albums filled with Polaroid film that has yellowed with the years. Or the strange sense that comes over me when I open the old tin that stores my great uncle Pete's belongings that date back to World War I. My great grandfather wrote letters to the family detailing his contracting work in California in the late Forties. Opening those envelopes— being careful not to rip them—is as sacred a family ritual as I could ever perform.

Needless to say, I don't feel the same torque on my heartstrings when I open my email, locate a file on a faraway server, or upload a picture to Facebook.

Take a moment to consider a picture frame.

A picture frame makes a picture so much more than a picture. Some of the greatest achievements in a life are encased between a matted piece of paper and a glass pane. That old picture of the great grandma you never met, a high school diploma, or a college degree, a professional certification, a wedding photo, and baby's first steps. Family vacations, or just a picture with friends from a long weekend out of town. They instantly mean more in a frame. Each framed picture is a slideshow all its own.

Take a moment to consider the old leather messenger bag your dad used on his paper route.

The leather may have started to crack by now, and most certainly has that familiar musty smell of all things old. If you look closely on the inside flap, you can see the ink stains still prevalent enough to make out the world "Times" forever emblazoned from years of morning rain and snow. It was in this bag that the town's news was transported to its citizens. Before he could throw a curveball or a perfect spiral, your old man learned to flip a paper onto Mrs. McCallister's front porch. He learned of the news of the day, and the importance of being informed. He learned the responsibility that went along with waking up early and performing a service that others depended on.

Take a moment to consider the scrapbook you made with your girlfriends from seventh grade. Inside its protective pages seal in the memories of the moments that shaped who you were back then, and who you've become now. Pictures of freckle-faced kids in sweatshirts with gap-toothed smiles. Those same chubby cheeks that have now given away to finely defined cheekbones and manicured eyebrows had to start somewhere. And it is under these pages, along with tickets to middle school dances and silly notes passed along in hallway bathrooms or between desks, that friendship can forever be preserved.

These physical documents mean so much more than a photo on Instagram, the "Front Page" on CNN, or even a slideshow set to music looping on a computer or tablet.

Computers are amazing things, but as document holders, they

could never hope to be as cool as their more physical counter-parts.

And, speaking of cool, no document holder has ever been as cool as the inside pocket on a suit jacket, or a sport coat.

Picture along with me the retired serviceman I saw the other day. He's in his late sixties and looks like he could still do two hundred crunches no problem. He wears a dark mock turtleneck with expertly tailored slacks, and maroon loafers. He wears a high-profile baseball style cap with the letters of his battalion stitched on the front in bright gold. He's sitting in a chair, and even though his pant legs extend rather high—almost all the way past his calf—as they bunch as he sit, his socks are pulled high enough so you don't see any of his bare skin. His facial features remind me of the actor Ed Harris, and on top of everything else, he's wearing a tight fitting sport coat.

I see him sitting in a bank of empty chairs in a public place, and very calmly he goes into the front inside pocket of his coat, and pulls out a long thin document. From my vantage point, I have no idea what it is, but he glances at it, looks up for a moment as if to think, and then calmly slides it back into his jacket pocket. I'm not sure if there's any way to accurately express just how cool he looked doing this. He then got up from his seat, buttoned the top button of his coat, and sauntered out of sight as if the scene was about to get exponentially less interesting now that he was no longer a part of it.

Think about a how many different things can come out of the inside pocket of a sport coat.

Your boss comes to give you two front row seats to opening night of Jay-Z at Madison Square Garden. Those tickets weren't just sitting in the back pocket of an old pair of dungarees.

Your real estate guy comes into a room, and without a word pulls out a single document that needs your signature to get you sole ownership of a new three flat in the trendy part of downtown. There will be a thousand other forms to sign, but they aren't the cool ones, and they don't get delivery via sport coat pocket.

A small town banker puts on his sport coat to make a house

call. He's wearing old jeans and boots, but it's a special occasion, so he throws on the coat for good measure. At your kitchen table, he pulls out a notice from inside his front pocket and hands it to your wife. She reads it and then her eyes well up with tears. The bank has decided to back the loan you've been needing, and this is the certified document that tells you that. A business envelope and a stamp would have done the trick, but this isn't first-class mail we're talking about here. This is sport coat class, the kind of news that can only be delivered in person, by the worthiest of individuals.

A Brad Pitt-like character walks up next to you in Vegas. Just as you've planned. You roll down a tinted window of your sports car, and from inside his front pocket he pulls out twenty five large in unmarked bills. You exchange the bills for a single piece of paper that he then places back into his front pocket without even looking at it. He motions for you to roll up your window, and just like that, the meeting is over. It might have been more secure to complete this transaction over an encrypted network somewhere between the Caymans, and Switzerland, but then you wouldn't have gotten to see the slight glance of approval over dark glasses that marks any transaction like the one described above, and come on, how cool is that?

An old man walks into a funeral parlor. He signs the guest book, nods to the hostess, and heads to the front of the room. The area is full of more flowers than he can remember seeing in a long time. He looks around briefly but doesn't focus on anything for longer than a second or two. The rest of the family will arrive soon, and he has a piece of business to attend to. He goes up to the open casket, and kneels down slowly as he begins to weep. He tells his wife of 52 years that he loves her and can't wait to see her again in heaven. Still kneeling, he pulls out a sealed envelope with a single letter "A" pressed in hard with blue pen from his coat pocket. He holds it in his hand for a few seconds, as if he's remembering every word he wrote. Then he quietly places the envelope in between the hands of woman in front of him. Not one set of human eyes will ever again read that letter, but I can assure you, its contents are pretty cool.

So hear me now, OfficeMax, in between the wireframe desktop organizers and the easels that hold really large canvases, put some sport coats in stock. 44R, I'll be by to pick one up on my way to my next big party. After all, I do want to be the coolest guy in the room...

Dishes are Done!

T he beginning of this piece may suggest that a more appropriate title for this entry should be, "Why Do Old Men Walk
around Naked in Locker Rooms?" but I promise that feeling
will only last a moment. While that is a topic that I often wonder
about, it is also a topic I'd rather not discuss at any great length. I
don't think anyone wants to read about it, and I surely don't wish
to hash it out any deeper than I already have...

Unclothed wanderers or not, I've never really been much of a
steam room or sauna guy at the gym. The thought of sitting on
wooden benches in a very warm room with a flock of other males
has just never really done it for me. I used to visit the sauna after
swimming sessions at LA Fitness where I once was a member.
Admittedly, my first reason for venturing into this dark, warm
room was out of sheer curiosity. A lot of other guys from the gym
really seemed to like it in there. What was all the fuss about?

Upon entering for the first time, I was greeted by the
expressionless acknowledgement that men often give each other
upon entering potentially awkward social situations. It's what I
like to call the, "Yes, I see that you're there, but beyond that, I
really don't see any other need to acknowledge you," look. And
when you think about it, why else would anyone do anything
more than that? It's not like you're going to go in and wave to
some random guy you don't know. Can you imagine being the
recipient of such a wave? "...Okay, someone just waved at me in
the sauna. Now what?" Similarly, the head nod isn't really even
necessary. I mean, after all, do you really want someone to notice
you while you're in this room?

Aside from the awkward entrance, there's the choice of seating
conundrum. Ideally, my thought was always to just sit as far away
from everyone as I could. With a bunch of men just sitting around,

there's really no need to crowd anyone. After all, the stated reason for entrance to one of these places is to relax, and I don't know about you, but I don't really take much relaxation from sitting overly close to someone I don't know. Throw in the heat, sweat, lack of clothing, etc., and it can really get awkward. There really should be a sauna attendant whose job it is to watch out for these things. You know, if the sauna is nearing capacity, this kind person could simply say, "You know what, I think now isn't the best time..."

Because letting the natural order of things play out as they would doesn't always work. Sometimes you go in, only to find out that the room is mostly full. Then what? Do you turn around and walk out? Not usually. So then you end up needing to make eye contact with someone to try and get them to slide over a few scootches for you. This maneuver is usually met with overall resentment. After all, a good relaxation session does not need to involve interruption to move. Or, there's always the chance that you run into the racquet ball duo who just finished a tough match. They are sitting overly close to each other, and depending on their age, may or may not be covering themselves with any sort of towel. While I may actually stand to learn something from Back Wall Bob, his serving strategy isn't really something I care to hear about at a moment like this. Personally, I'd love it if he could pick up that towel next to him and spare me any further indecent exposure.

So between not really wanting to ask others to move, and not really wanting to nestle up next to Bob and Rob, seating is just a hassle. And then, if you do happen to find a good place to sit, what happens next really isn't all that relaxing.

Perhaps enjoyment of this 175 degree hot box requires a certain mindset that I just don't have, or maybe my internal organs were predisposed not to enjoy such extreme temperatures, but whatever the case, after about twelve seconds in the sauna, I'm usually to the point where I want to come out. My heart always feels like someone is stepping on it, and while I always seem to want to sweat, it's as if my pores try really hard not to let any perspiration escape. Soon after, though, they always seem to relent, and I end up sitting in a quickly forming puddle of grossness.

Every once in a while, I would end up seeing someone I knew in the sauna upon entering. But if you don't go sit next to this person immediately, you get yourself into another pickle. I've never heard anyone conduct a conversation from side wall to side wall in the sauna. Calling across the room above the noise of the heater just isn't something you do. There's some sort of unwritten code. Nothing more than a 12-inch voice in the sauna.

Mental exhaustion was far more often the result of these sauna sessions, to the point where I just threw in the towel. The only good part of the sauna experience to me was the ten seconds of cool air I would feel upon exit of the little room back into the "normal" temperature of the rest of the locker room.

I haven't been in a sauna in a few years, and I don't miss it one bit. Partially because I found a new solution that doesn't involve nearly as much social interaction. In fact, this practice is also quite useful around the house. When I need to relax, I just do the dishes!

How exactly is doing the dishes relaxing you ask?

Well, I'm a dishwasher user, and as any dishwasher user knows, if you put dishes into the dishwasher, you also have to take them out. And my friends, this is the best part! After my Normal dishwashing cycle ends, I anxiously await some of the heated drying process to take place. Before it can ever finish completely, I love to open the dishwasher door. Placing myself so that my head is directly above the gap I'm about to create when opening the door, my head is in perfect position to receive the forthcoming gift.

And that gift is glorious.

Upon unlatching the dishwasher door, steam comes rushing out of the warm compartment. It billows into my flared nostrils, and engulfs my face. For a few brief moments, the warmth from the steam radiates through the entire upper half of my body. In the next few seconds, as nearly all the steam has escaped from the dishwasher, the warmth starts to make its way down to the rest of my body. Right about the time the dishwasher stops emitting steam, the warming effect reaches my feet. For a brief moment or two, my entire body is warm. My sinuses have quickly been cleared, and a refreshing feeling comes over me that no sauna could ever provide. I usually make sure to wear my glasses during this ordeal. Having them fog up to the point where visibility in my own kitchen is approximately two inches is a bonus.

Why go sit in a sweaty sauna when you can stand in your kitchen feeling rejuvenated lemony fresh after only eight seconds? No hairy fat guys, no racquetball strategy, no possibility of a towel malfunction, and no feeling like your heart is about to beat out of your chest.

Just a quick steam treatment in the comfort of your own kitchen. Thank you, Maytag, I've never felt better.

Now go, try this immediately. Even if you don't like it, at least your dishes will be clean at the end of the process!

Feeling Bad for Party Food

I attended a housewarming party recently, and had a great time. My friends were excited to have people to their new place, and it was a nice opportunity to meet some new people. The house was festively decorated, there were sporting events to watch, and of course, great food to eat! The theme of this party was "Tailgate Food," which was an excellent idea.

Menu items included BBQ pulled chicken sliders, homemade chili, jalapeno popper dip, queso dip, bratwurst, sausages, hot dogs, and two desserts that I hear were out of this world. The first dessert was a fresh batch of Rice Krispie treats, and the second was some sort of cocoa cluster surprise that went flying off the serving dish so fast I swear there must have been a narcotic in the recipe.

I surveyed the scene, and there wasn't a face in the room that wasn't full of jubilation. SEC football gave way to ACC football, stories were shared, and common ground was established. I learned that one couple has a 185 lb. dog, one of the guys at the party was a proud member of the Nashville Fire Department, and that a nearby apartment complex had a pretty substantial problem with the Brown Recluse spider. All in all it was a terrific night...

...Until I spotted a large bowl of fruit on the corner of the counter in the kitchen. It was full to the brim. It looked as though no one had yet touched it. This was appalling. There were mounds of strawberries, green melon, grapes, even kiwi! This was like a treasure trove of snacking possibility, and it was like nobody cared. Overshadowed by the more savory tailgate dishes, the fruit bowl was being swallowed up by neglect.

I have a soft spot in my heart for the fruit bowl. I love fruit, and more times than not, guests do not have the food pyramid in mind when they put their party hats on (There wasn't a veggie platter present at this particular shindig, but if there had been, you can bet I would have been slamming baby carrots like there was no tomorrow.). Perhaps more peculiar, I have a soft spot for any dish that doesn't seem to be getting any love in the midst of any get-together.

I mean, when someone has the courage to bring unsalted pita chips to a party, I can't just let them go untouched. Somewhere, somehow, someone thought it'd be a good idea to bring those babies. How bad would they feel if they left the party, and the bag was unopened? That's a hit to their psyche I just can't let happen.

Spinach quiche. Downright awful tasting, but I'll gladly portion out a microscopic sliver if it means the person who brought it didn't have to experience the humiliation of bringing a dish that drew less interest than Pat Buchanan in a presidential election. One could easily ask why someone would bring date bars to a party under any circumstance, but what good does that do? In that situation, you take one for the date bar maker, and you force that baby down the gullet. I realized the other night when I was eating the equivalent to my third whole kiwi that maybe I was being a little hyper-sensitive.

People probably don't really care if their bag of pita chips gets opened or not. In fact, maybe they even like it. Chances are they like pita chips, and if the bag doesn't get opened, they can easily take it back home like it was never even at the party in the first place. Genius. In that case, I'm going to start bringing my favorite foods that no one likes to all the parties I go to. Watch out friends, dark red kidney beans and the little square boxes of Brussels sprouts are coming to a fiesta near you (Boxed Brussels sprouts are the best.)!

And then I realized something else. Is most cases where I eat unwanted foods at parties, I don't even know the person who made the dish. This got me to thinking, do I feel bad for the person making the food, or am I actually feeling bad for the food itself? After all, a sad-looking deviled egg looks pretty, well, sad. A wilted salad with no dressing looks awfully depressing, and a flat corn soufflé looks an awful lot like it's had a bad day...

So please friends, now that I have come out as an unwanted party food sympathizer, keep it mind before our next soiree. Because the only thing worse than eating spinach quiche is nobody eating spinach quiche.

YES, I Hadn't Thought about That in Years!

T hroughout the process of writing this book, I've spent a lot of time thinking about how I think. Of course, I've realized that sometimes I overthink. I almost never underthink, and I rarely understand why I think how I do. But, I've decided that this is awesome. I love my brain, no matter how ridiculous it is sometimes!

One thing I'd love to know are the stimuli that trigger me to think the way I do. Well, maybe I don't really want to know, but there are some crazy examples of my brain at work throughout this book that could use some further explanation. For many of these strange occurrences, I could probably trace something back to a root if I really thought about it long enough.

I had broccoli for dinner last month, and the next thing I knew I was thinking of an Easter egg hunt. Now, most people probably wouldn't associate those two in any sort of halfway coherent thought. But, here's how it happened. I overcooked my broccoli in the microwave, so I thought about getting some fresh broccoli to steam. And then, while thinking of fresh broccoli I just wanted to go to the grocery store so I could get any kind of vegetable that comes wrapped up in a produce rubber band. I LOVE produce rubber bands. Their consistency is terrific, they stretch just the right amount, and in a non-stretched state, they are the perfect size to fit over my boney little wrists. It always surprises me when I get one of these little blue beauties wrapped around a large floret of broccoli. It's far more necessary when bundling green onions, or asparagus, as those foods can actually escape without them. But, you know what, I'm not one to complain, the more of these rubber bands I have, the better!

So from the veggie rubber band, I immediately began an internal argument with myself, "Is the veggie rubber band darker or lighter in color than a robin's egg?" After all, if I were ever going to want to describe my favorite rubber band to someone else, I'd want to be able to accurately refer to the distinctive blue hue it generally possesses. After about two seconds of contemplation, I realized that Robin's Egg Blue was nowhere near Veggie Rubber Band Blue (Author's Note: If anything, Veggie Rubber Band Blue is closer to racquetball blue, but even that isn't 100% accurate a comparison.).

No matter the actual color at this point, my mind was flying in a completely different direction. Robin eggs gave way to the speckled chocolate candy that I used to get in my Easter basket as a kid. Sometimes these were larger malted milk balls, but mostly they were the small, poppable size that simply had a hard candy shell. From there, it's probably pretty easy to guess how I got from Easter candy to an Easter egg hunt, and the odyssey through my brain can take a break for a second.

From broccoli to an Easter egg hunt, in a few short steps. If only this kind of thinking was acceptable when I was doing proofs in high school geometry. See Mrs. Craine, it all DID make sense!

As you can see, it doesn't take much to make a connection in my head, so I think that's why it's even that much more surprising when I surprise myself.

Today, for the first time in at least ten years, I found myself thinking about the Toyota Previa mini-van. If you're not familiar with a Previa, Toyota brought this baby to market in 1990 as a more modern alternative to the ultra-boxy Dodge Caravan that had come out four years earlier. At the time, I'm sure the Previa's rounded-edge styling was seen as futuristic as anything anyone had ever dreamed of, but as time has passed, history has not been kind to the Previa. If you happen to see one today, you'll swear it looks more like Humpty Dumpty on wheels than something that was ever viewed as fashion forward.

As a rule, I love mini-vans. I can't tell you why. My mom never had one growing up, and my dad would surely lose a small amount of my respect for me if I had ever voiced that opinion around him. Society certainly doesn't glorify mini-vans in the media, especially not to twentysomething males! But I'm not in the market for a new car, and I haven't seen anyone recently that owns, has owned, or plans to own a mini-van. I haven't recently been watching a TV show that featured one, or a book, nor had I see one in an old picture. In fact, despite my love for the official vehicle of socermomdom, I never liked the Previa to begin with. In fact, I always thought their shape was better suited to be a part of a matryoshka doll set than an automobile.

I think two of my friends' moms had a Previa growing up, but at the time of my thought, I hadn't been interacting with, or thinking about them in any way. I sat on my couch for like three minutes—an eternity in brain time—and tried to connect the dots. Why the Previa? Why now? The body style changed in 1996, I hadn't seen one in who knows how long, and I even had to Google the name of the Previa to make sure it was what I thought it was when the name first popped into my head.

At that moment, I was on my couch, reading a book about minor league baseball from an era that was before the Previa came out. I hadn't been out driving recently, and I can't even remember the last time I saw a mini-van of any kind driving around Nashville. Even soccer moms drive SUVs now...

After my three minute brain scan, I got this huge grin in my face. Somehow, the Toyota Previa had entered my brain. I had no idea how or why. No triggers. No connections. Just a random thought.

And now, I had a huge smile on my face. How awesome is that?

Acceptable Topics
of Conversation
with Your Hairdresser

L et me preface this by saying I'm a SuperCuts-with-a-coupon kind of guy when it comes to getting haircuts. I know for a lot of people out there—especially women—the hairdresser is a trusted confidant, or a friend of many years. For me, I have never planned out a haircut more than an hour in advance, nor have I ever requested my hair be done by anyone other than Ms. First Available (Despite what you might have heard about her, she's not bad.). So to say that my relationship might be different with my hairdresser than yours is with yours, that's fine, at least you know where I'm coming from.

My goals are pretty simple when I walk into a hair "salon." Author's Note: Salon is usually a loose term when you're in a SuperCuts. I try to get in and get out as fast as possible, and I try and make it known to Ms. FA that her job is to make sure that I don't have to return any time soon. I realize this may be as insensitive as telling the checkout lady at Hallmark that you work for eCards.com, or something, but I'm always honest and up front with them at least. I've found that there's no better way than to endear yourself to someone you've never met than telling them, "Okay, I don't want to have to be back here any time soon, chop my mop nice and short, ya here?"

As you might have been gathering throughout these pages, I find talking and sharing thoughts to come pretty easily. I'll tell pretty much anybody anything in any setting. And yet, I never really know what to say to hairdressers.

The last time I was in to get a mop chop, the lady cutting my hair (an FA whose name was actually Abby) had a picture of her son taped to the mirror. Before I knew what I was saying, I heard myself asking her if that was her "little nugget up there on the mirror." She laughed at my word choice, and you could tell she was taken aback a little bit by my calling her son a nugget. Nonetheless, the boy on the mirror was her son, and she spent a few seconds telling me how awesome he was. This was nice, as I could tell she was a loving mother, but it was only a brief distraction before she turned the question on me, "So do you have any kids?"

"No...No I don't." Dead end. The kids topic is always a dead end. I'm not a father, I'm not an uncle, I don't have any cousins that I see on a regular basis under the age of eleven, and thus am pretty useless when a young mom wants to talk about her toddler. I once told a hairdresser that I used to be a toddler once. I don't think that was really a good idea. She somehow managed to finish cutting my hair without looking at me for the next ten minutes. She gave me this awful stare when I got out of the chair, as if to say, "Okay creep, I hope you enjoy your haircut, see you never again." Personally, I didn't see the problem with saying I used to be a toddler once. Sure, maybe it came off as being creepy, but I'm almost certain just about anyone that had ever sat in her chair was a toddler at one point, so I really don't think that's fair. Either way, I try and avoid the kid topic as much as possible.

Next in the hairdresser handbook for continuing conversation with your client must be "talk about their weekend." Now, I'm not sure how it always seems to happen this way, but I always seem to get my hair cut on Tuesdays after I did nothing the weekend before. It never fails. I get the question, "Did you do anything fun this weekend?" and the results are usually pretty pitiful. Ninety-nine percent of the time, that answer is a resounding "No." The last time I was in and got this question, I distinctly remember having gotten really excited that past weekend because I had successfully washed socks and had exactly zero mis-mates. Now, this is a HUGE occasion in my life, but general social norms tell me that this may not be best thing to talk about with 23-year-old women when they ask you about your weekend. By default, I usually have to say something like, "Oh yeah, you know, just needed to take it easy and rest up." To this comment, First Available Tami usually says, "Oh yeah, big night out on Friday downtown?" Of course my first thought usually is, "Does walking on the treadmill and then checking my mail count as a big Friday night?" but my response is usually something like, "Oh yeah, you know..." Most of the time, I don't have to explain any further, but it usually makes for another pretty uneventful next eight minutes while she finishes up my cut.

Since relocating to Tennessee, the topic of where I live, what I think of the area, and where I'm from has come up a lot more than it ever did before the move. But this topic has some landmines, too. I usually get my hair cut at lunch time near where my client's office is. This area is about thirty minutes from where I live, and the area where I live is most famous for being the historical site of former president Andrew Jackson. I tried this topic with First Available Tami, and she informed me that she'd gone to see Jackson's home on a field trip in grade school. By all accounts, she thought it was super LAME. I figured it probably wasn't the best time to tell her that when I had gone to that same site, my grandpa and I had blissfully spent fifteen minutes in the parking lot counting out of state license plates. If she thought the site was lame, she might have described this game as "dorktastic."

If the stylist is to find out I'm from the Chicago area, she usually wants to talk about the city itself. Now, don't get me wrong, I'm a fan of Chicago, but I'm actually not much of a tourist when it comes to having done a lot of cool things. I'm pretty sure every hairdresser who's ever visited Chicago has taken an architectural boat tour down the Chicago River. I lived in Chicagoland for more than twenty five years, and would you guess the one thing I haven't done? Of course! I have never taken the architectural boat tour. Upon hearing this, I inevitably get lumped into the "boring Chicagoan" category, and that topic ends.

With older stylists, I ask about their families, and that's never good. Their kids are either a handful, their sister is feuding with the rest of the family, or the worst of all: the Mother Who Just Fell and Hurt Something. I will try to politely listen and offer support in this situation, but it becomes one of those conversations where I offer a lot of, "That's tough" or "Oh man, I hope she's feeling better." I actually don't mind being a sounding block for these people, but it seems like every time we go down that road, the poor lady ends up nearly in tears with their situation.

I've tried sports, and let's just say we're usually on different wavelengths when it comes to this topic.

I've tried breaching the topic of SuperCuts continued investment in racing sponsorship. You can imagine how that goes...

I've asked about whether or not they enjoy the SuperCuts mobile app. Apparently, a lot of people check in on the app, and then never come to the store. That's about a thirty-second conversation.

I try and talk about when their shift will end. The answer is never soon enough, so that's a big old dud sandwich.

My job as an industrial marketer for tools and machinery also isn't a big area of interest to young females. Imagine that!

I don't have any tattoos, nor do I plan on getting any...Strike sixteen with First Available Tami...I also don't have a dog, nor do I do yoga or Pilates.

Over the years, I've decided I probably have more in common with most convicted felons than I do with most SuperCuts Scissor Spinners.

So to answer the question, for me, the only appropriate topic of conversation with my hairdresser is the weather. That's one thing you've got to love about people, felons or hairdressers, everyone can relate to sunny and 75!

Toy Dinosaurs

I recently found out that Barbie is turning 55 next year. I've got to say, she's still looking pretty good for 54 ½. I remember while I was watching "Toy Story 3" how cool it was that Barbie was still relevant in the toy market all these years later. She still had a prominent role in the movie, and the idea of Barbie and Ken is still one that resonates with any generation. Unlike many toys that come and go, Barbie seems to have withstood the test of time. During a recent breeze through the Target toy aisle, I still saw Barbie all over the place, and a little girl with a new pink box in her hand while she sat in the cart. Target.com lists 277 Barbie-related items, and even gives the little blonde doll her own personalized landing page (For those of us in the website building business, that's a big deal.). Not bad for a platinum blonde who could easily qualify for her AARP card.

Barbie really is a perfect toy. It allows young girls to play make believe, they can play dress up, make Barbie wear all sorts of different outfits, and learn about all sorts of occupations with all of the different types of Barbies. I'm sure there are scholars out there who have linked Barbies to materialism, self-image issues, or whatever else academics try to link to good honest fun. For the sake of this argument, let's remember, I'm not a researcher, and academic, nor am I a girl. I have no idea if Barbies are actually good or bad for a young girl. Girls seem to like them, though, and they've been around for a long time, so I'm going to give them the benefit of the doubt.

With all of that being said, it makes perfect sense why Barbie would remain popular for more than five decades. Dolls have been around for centuries, and Barbie puts the quintessential American spin on the doll.

There is one toy that has been around for longer than Barbie that I really can't figure out, and that is the toy dinosaur.

Dinosaurs have been extinct for 66 million years, and yet, somehow they have endured, and are still a popular kids' toy today. By comparison, they aren't as popular as Barbie—"Dinosaur" only has 61 search result items at Target.com—but even that many is pretty impressive.

Think about that for a second. Kids are playing with a toy that represents a species of animals that hasn't been around since the end of the Mesozoic Era! Barbie has had a good run, and she was born during the Eisenhower administration...

I did some research in why this is, because it is a fascinating idea to me that kids for generations have been playing with toys that depict creatures that no one on earth has ever seen. As you might expect, dinosaurs first appeared in classic literature. Dickens, Jules Verne, Sir Arthur Conan Doyle, and then later in films like "King Kong" and "Godzilla." In recent memory, Michael Crichton's "Jurassic Park" series revitalized interest in the prehistoric beasts.

But even those are only a few examples of ties to creatures that haven't been around for 65 million years.

I suppose that it's possible the fact that scientists made discoveries regarding dinosaurs right before they first appeared in literature might have something to do the fact that they caught on. Science can be a driver for what assimilates into popular culture. Although, why the dinosaur? Electrons were also discovered around the same time dinosaurs were, and you haven't seen kids playing with electron models for the last 150 years!

What else is as old as dinosaurs that still exists today?

Carbon?

Water?

Green plants?

Not exactly a list of things that are going to get a kid excited at birthday party time...

Oh thanks Aunt Louis, you got me a fern!

Aunt Edith, you shouldn't have, I have too much carbon as it is...

Mom, thanks a lot for another bottle of water this year, I can't wait to mix in some Gatorade powder...

And yet the dinosaur wins out.

The "Jurassic Park" movies made almost $2 billion worldwide, and there's another one coming in 2015. From that spawned action figures, video games, carnival rides, and even stuffed animals.

Funny to think a kid would want to sleep with a fuzzy likeness of a 100-ton carnivore!

It really is unfathomable.

Although, if I learned anything during my childhood, if it made sense in "Toy Story," it's probably safe not to question it.

One of Andy's toys in Toy Story is a green dinosaur named Rex. Oh, and he's friends with Barbie, too. Of course.

Obscure Prized Possessions

It would be hard for me to come up with just one item that I would consider my most near and dear worldly possession. And if I were really being technical about it, my most prized possessions are probably relationships I have with family and friends, but of the things on earth that would be close to the top, pretty much all of them are obscure.

I don't know if there's a quiz out there in Cosmo that says, "What do your prized possessions say about you?" but I'd be interested to read it if there was one.

I'd be willing to bet that if you took a poll of all the people who claim to have prized possessions, their items would fit at least some of the following criteria:

- The item has to be rare—A diamond, a one-of a kind collectable, a uniquely made, or uniquely designed piece that you can't just get anywhere

- The item has to have a personal connection—I would be willing to venture a guess that most prized possessions are closely linked to a relationship with someone, something, or a shared experience that involved someone close

- The item has to be tied to a timeframe in the life of its owner that is significant in some way or another

A first car may fit this bill because it is linked to the important timeframe of growing up and becoming an adult. Or maybe because you worked on it with your dad, and it reminded you of him. Or maybe in the years since you first got it, a 1968 K5 Blazer has become more and more rare, and owning one gets more significant as the years go by.

It's difficult to judge people by the type of things they cherish. And really, who am I to say what's important to someone else, but in general, I think I relate more closely to people who cherish the smaller things in life. After all, this is a book about little things...

But my point is if someone's prized possession in life is a brand new Mercedes, I'm not sure they're really my type of person. Again, to stop short of judging, it very easily could have been someone's goal in life to work hard enough to one day be able to buy a new Mercedes, and the fact that they own one could be the culmination of a dream they set with their dad on his death bed. I can't possibly know, nor am I in any place to judge.

But I will say, I think the more obscure the item, the more fun.

On Christmas Day 1999, I received a rather inauspicious Christmas present from my Aunt Kim. In our family, we affectionately refer to my Aunt Kim as "Aunt Socks." Why you ask? Well, Aunt Kim for many years gave socks to nearly every family member on gift giving occasions. As a young kid, I didn't really like this very much. Before you even opened your gift, the thoughts were already going through your head..."Oh great, here's another pair of socks. I can't wait to see what color..."

And yet, on Christmas of '99 I opened one heck of a pair of socks. A pair of socks that changed the way I think about socks, gifts and life.

Let me explain.

As you'll recall from my earlier list, one of the ways an item can secure itself as a prized possession is to be relevant during an important time in one's life.

Well, at the time I received this gift, there was nothing more important in the world than the pending Y2K crisis. Somehow, the world was all in a tizzy because everyone was worried that if the world's computers and accounting systems couldn't account for the year being 2000 instead of 19--, the whole world was going to implode.

Conspiracy theorists and contrarians anxiously awaited the impending doom.

Analysts all over TV were offering their predictions on what was going to happen, and many people in the general public were running to bulk food stores and stocking up on gallons of water dehydrated food. Nuclear bomb? No, potential computer glitch.

Of course, as with any good global overreaction, there were plenty of people out to capitalize on the situation. Y2K merchandise was all the rage, and before I knew it, Aunt Socks made sure I had a pair of Y2K gym socks!

The world was set to end and all, but at least I could spend my last days in comfort, and if I wanted to be sure to be fit for the apocalypse, I could work out in style with a solid pair of mid-calf level, logo-ed socks!

Just what I'd always wanted! I'm trying to think back on whether or not "hokey gag socks" were on my Christmas list that year...I'm thinking...yeah, no.

And yet for some reason when I got them, I remember having this huge smile on my face. I was in the prime of my teenage years at this point, and more so than at any point in my life, image was everything to me. On any other day, in any other setting, I would have scoffed at these socks and prayed that none of my friends even found out about them.

But there was something about the smile on my Aunt Kim's face, and that brought out the second necessity in creating a potential prized possession: a connection to a relationship in life that is important.

My Aunt Kim in many ways is a role model for me, despite us being about as different as two human beings could possibly be. I see a lot of the person I've become in who she is and always has been in her life. She's someone who I never felt was ashamed of any part of who she was. Internally, I'm sure there were struggles just like we all have struggles, but externally, they didn't show. Growing up I saw a unique individual who wasn't afraid to display that for family and friends. She gave us socks for Christmas every year and somehow made that fun! She made crazy birthday cakes, and even had a phase where she was into making denim purses...Again, not really my thing...But I so enjoyed her spirit, and her approach, and I think I get some of my love for obscurity from her. Y2K socks are so her. In every way imaginable. Every time I wear them, I think of her.

And that brings me to the last awesome part about my Y2K socks. I still wear them. Going on fourteen years later, they don't come nearly as high up my leg these days, and the elastic at the top is a bit worn out, but I still wear them. I'm fully aware that one day I may wear a hole in the heel, but I don't really believe in not gaining enjoyment from something just because there's a chance something might go wrong. I don't normally wear them in public when I'm wearing shorts...but in no way am I afraid to bust those babies out. It's amazing that after such a long time, they don't have holes in them. I'm sure they were purchased at some gag store, or gift shop somewhere, and yet the quality of these socks has been unbelievable.

The rarity and obscurity of an item like this really seals for me how much the socks mean to me. With every passing year, I can look back on the whole Y2K fiasco, and laugh. And, every year it gets to be one year further into history, and it gives me a chance to reflect on my life.

Thinking back to those last days in 1999, where after months of disregarding Y2K as a hoax, my mom finally decided at the eleventh hour that we needed to prepare ourselves in case something happened. So what did we do? We went out and gathered three gallons of water and put them into our deep freeze in the basement. Because, of course, three gallons of water will most definitely sustain a family of four in the midst of a global disaster...

Or maybe the most current reflection. What would someone think if they saw me—late twentysomething marketing executive—working out on an elliptical wearing socks that proclaimed that I was Property of Y2K? People don't exactly walk into an apartment complex workout facility and expect to see that every day. I know I'd do a double take if I was next to me on the elliptical. "Is that guy really wearing socks that say 'Property of Y2K?'"

Yes sir. Yes I am. And they are awesome!

Sharing Fear

I n January 1933, Franklin Roosevelt delivered his famous inaugural speech in which he told a weary nation in the midst of the Great Depression that "The only thing to fear... is fear itself." The speech went on to last twenty minutes, but those first few lines have gone down in history as some of the most powerful lines an American politician has ever uttered.

I think at the time those words were as well-timed as any that have ever been uttered. As a nation, our people probably needed a pep talk. We probably all got collectively out over our skis in the Roaring Twenties, and the Great Depression served as a most unfortunate nationwide reality check. Roosevelt proved to be the type of forward-thinking leader to bring the country through the tough times.

I don't totally agree with him about having nothing to fear, though...

Squirrels are very scary. So is any large rodent that scurries unexpectedly. Giving blood, the potential to lose large amounts of blood in any fashion, and needles in general. All very real things worthy of very real fears.

Yes, I'm afraid of squirrels—and horses, and rats, mice, raccoons and you name it—and I realize that these are not the same fears that FDR was referring to in the wake of the Depression.

There were very real fears back then, too. How about having food, running water, heat in the winter? Much more real fears than my silly fears of small animals I could easily just step on if they ever decided to "charge" me.

But I think that what Roosevelt was saying is that fear becomes unmanageable when fear is internalized. As a nation, we needed to stare the fearful realities in the eye, and challenge them. We needed to start programs to create jobs, we needed to subsidize our farmers to grow food, etc.

In essence, we were all just sharing our collective fears. The harsh reality of widespread drought and joblessness didn't disappear overnight, the nation was just distracted building new roads and bridges.

In a similar way, I think people need to be more open about sharing their fears.

When I was little, I rode a horse. I don't remember it being too terribly traumatic. When I got a little older, I rode one again at camp. The horse didn't move, I was the slowest kid, and when I dismounted the horse, I fell awkwardly, and some of the other kids laughed at me. For the next fifteen years, I kept mum on horses. I tried never to say anything about them, tried as deftly as I could to avoid having to discuss them, ride them, or do anything that had to do with horses. Inside, I became more and more frightened by them. Simply over internalizing my thoughts on horses, I went from having one mildly bad experience with them, to all the sudden being deathly afraid of them. A few months ago, I made it public to some friends that I was scared of horses. They laughed at first, but they soon suggested that we go horseback riding sometime soon. I could barely stomach the suggestion, but I thought at least if I could look at some pictures of horses being friendly that would help. It did. In the weeks that have followed, I've talked with more people about my fear, and with each time that I do, it seems as though I have less and less anxiety about the whole subject.

I'm sure it will be a different story in a few weeks when my plans to go horseback riding come to fruition, but as of right now, I'm feeling good!

Think back to some of the most fearful times in your life.

When you were learning to ride a bike, you didn't know yet to internalize your fears. You said, "Mommy hold on still, don't let me fall" because you didn't want to fall. In third grade when you didn't understand fractions, you told your teacher you didn't get it. You weren't yet scared enough of being wrong, and your teacher explained it to you.

And then, middle school hit, and there were literally too many new things and too many new people all at the same time. Even if you felt comfortable sharing everything that was new that you didn't understand, there wouldn't be enough time in the day. All of the sudden kids were trying to be know-it-alls, talking about everything with your mom wasn't cool, and it didn't seem as easy to ask "dumb" questions in class.

It was at times like these that a lot of people learned to internalize things. They stopped sharing, and things got a whole lot more awkward.

By the time high school and college rolled around, a lot of this fear still existed, but by then we as people had learned how to divert our attention away from the matters at hand and bond over other issues. It became real easy to protest certain issues, or lose ourselves in a frosty beverage or two, but in many cases the majority of people continued to hide from their fears rather than face them.

As an adult it's hard to say, "I'm afraid of _____."

As a parent that's hard, too, I would think.

As a teacher, it's hard to say, "I don't have the answer."

As a coach, your team looks to you for answers, not fears. The halftime speech in the Super Bowl isn't about being afraid of losing, it's to go out there and WIN!

At work, as a community leader, and in relationships, it's not the natural thing to say, "I'm scared" or "I'm afraid."

But then what happens when we fail or come up short?

After the fact, when it doesn't matter as much, we admit to being afraid.

The executive of a company who after being fired says, "Well, I didn't want to do X, because I was afraid of Y..."

Or the coach who admits he was scared of the other team's star player...only after that player torches his team for six touchdowns or 50 points or something.

The divorce rate in the United States is roughly 14 for every 1,000 marriages in a given year. Over time, this equates to roughly half of the married population ending up divorced. Don't ask me how that math works out, but trust me, that's how they measure these things. In 1963, only 2.3 out of every 1,000 marriages ended in divorce.

So somehow over the last 50 years, Americans are now seven times more likely to get divorced now than they were in 1963. Is love that much more elusive now? Are people just generally becoming more and more incompatible? Married couples in 2013 are on average more educated than married couples in 1963, and the average age upon getting married is older. Wouldn't this seem to point to maturity, stability and thus longevity in a relationship?

Apparently not. And, I'd be willing to bet it has a lot to do with not sharing fear. Society has such a hard time admitting there is something they're having a hard time with, that they'd rather fail than face their fears.

I'm guilty of this in many arenas.

Heck, I've spent years being afraid of horses and field mice...

Fear is difficult. Fear alludes to imperfection, and there are few things harder than public decrees of imperfection. But hiding fear doesn't work. Think of middle school. Using fear as a tactic doesn't work either. Think of the Cold War (The United States didn't win the Cold War when it ended; the Soviet Union just stopped losing.).

Roosevelt did what Herbert Hoover couldn't—he put measures in place for people to be able to share their fears. Under the guise of reconstruction, our nation faced our fears, and we rebuilt each other, together, sharing the burden.

So, Mr. Roosevelt, I think what you meant to say was, "The only thing we have to fear is not sharing our fear with each other!"

Although, I think for the sake of our country, I'm glad he went with his wording. It sounds a lot better!

Context

OMBS AWAY!!
In a water balloon fight, or jumping off a diving board, "Bombs Away" may as well be the official tagline of summer fun.

In a small hallway bathroom in suburban America, "Bombs Away" may draw a wry smile and a sigh of relief from an exhausted mother of three as her youngest bids farewell to the living proof that he's finally potty trained...

On an aircraft carrier in the Middle East, "Bombs Away" may immediately trigger feelings of anxiety as a group of servicemen await with baited breath to see what happens next.

And I don't need to tell you what "Bombs Away" means if you decide to yell it in the middle of an airport...You may as well just keep running if that's what you're going to do...

Context is an amazing concept, and one of my favorite.

Sidenote: It seems weird to say I have a list of favorite concepts. I mean, I really do love the concept of waking up and thus not being tired anymore. Or eating and thus being full. Those are good concepts. I like the concept of speaking and then being spoken to, but to say something is one of my favorite concepts is rather strange. Even for me...

Context makes things so funny, and it can also make things so awkward.

I was in the clubhouse of my apartment complex today doing some writing on a report for work. I've been in this room many times, but for the first time, I noticed a watercolor painting of one of the buildings within the apartment complex. Naturally, this made a lot of sense. The complex probably commissioned a painter to paint one of the buildings as a nice "homey" touch for the residents of the complex. You know, a subtle way to remind the residents that they live in the ideal community in their area! And, if you don't believe them, check out this terrific painting!

The painting actually isn't bad...I kind of like it. But now imagine it at a high-end gallery in Midtown Manhattan! In your best snooty art gallery director's voice, say it with me now, "And here we have a beautiful contemporary piece. It's is entitled 'Manufactured Dwellings with Easy to Clean White Plastic Fencing All Around.' It is from a new art-eest, and we'll open the bidding at...oh say...$16.25."

In this scenario, you might see some little cheese plates fall to the ground in disbelief that such a painting on such a topic would dare enter such a rarefied gallery.

Now imagine seeing this painting as a 41 year-old man. You're at your kitchen table, and your nine year-old son has just brought you this masterpiece and proclaimed he's figured out his life's calling as a "Residential Rendering Specialist." Think of that stumble sandwich that all the sudden just got shoved in your mouth...

"Well of course, Jeffy, you can...uh...be anything you want... even if that means you're an apartment building paint—"

"NO Dad, Residential Rendering Specialist!"

"....Sure thing, kid. Yeah, that..."

And those are just a few instances. Imagine an old man who found this artwork 50 years after he had moved from the complex. Or the grieving son who came every day to walk his now-deceased mother's dog. That picture—as random as it may be, could be the lifeline that keeps them going.

To a bunch of hipster kids in a college town, it could be the perfect gag gift to hang in their apartment that looks nothing like this complex.

Context is everything in life.

It keeps you out of trouble when your wife knows the lipstick on your collar is actually hers...

It gets you into trouble when you post an innocent picture "enjoying the lake" on social media...when you're supposed to be at home on a sick day from work.

It brings you to tears if the full carton of milk means another day that your sick child hasn't eaten...

Or it can lift your spirits if you find a remnant of your lost dog's collar by a tree in the woods.

Context is what gives life greater meaning. A red car is just a red car, until that red car is a '63 Impala parked outside your old man's garage, waiting to reunite after 40 years apart.

A song is just a song, until it's "our song," the one from your first date or your honeymoon.

There are a lot of people who can throw a football 50 yards, and land it in a trash can, if that trashcan is sitting in the middle of a windless field on a random Tuesday. Doing that with 300-pound men chasing you, with 50 million people watching you on Super Bowl Sunday...That's what makes someone Drew Brees...

I think context is the greatest lesson someone can learn in life. And, I'm still learning it right now.

When the situation calls for calm, can you be calm?

When the boardroom needs a joke, can you sense it and deliver something with class?

When someone asks a rhetorical question, do you get the message?

When that look on your mom's face says something's wrong, can you sense it?

When it's best not to call that girl from the bar at 3 a.m., do you call her?

I'd be willing to bet that the most successful people in life—however you want to measure that—are the people who can successfully judge the context of a situation, and act accordingly.

So, if you're a young mother, and you know your kid is a "Bombs Away" kid... It's probably not the best idea to work on potty training at the airport!

All That for That?

I spend a lot of time at Midway Airport. My family lives in Chicago. I fly into Chicago often for work, and Southwest has its Chicago hub there. A perfect trifecta to lure me away from the much more crowded terminals of Chicago's other airport, O'Hare.

At the very end of the ticketing concourse at Midway sits a place that for some reason holds mythical value in my mind: the ticketing booth of Porter Airlines.

Who?

Yes, that's right, Porter Airlines.

I'm decently savvy on brands, companies, and business ventures, but I remember a few years back I started seeing this booth down at the end of the ticketing lobby. My curiosity sensors were flashing off the charts. Who are these Porter Airlines people? Why have I not heard of them?

And then, almost inexplicably, I immediately became enthralled with the idea of taking a flight on Porter Airlines.

It's a hard phenomenon to describe, but it's almost as if your curiosity just gets in the way of anything reasonable. I had no idea where Porter flew, nor did I care. I just wanted to fly Porter Airlines, really badly. Unfortunately for my curiosity craving, I'm a bit of an out-of-sight-out-of-mind person, and after leaving Midway, I forgot to look up Porter, and almost as quickly as the urge had stricken me, it was out of my mind.

...Until the next time I was at Midway, and this time, upon seeing the Porter sign behind their ticketing counter, I got mad.

Not mad like I was going to go up and throw my half eaten apple at them, but mad at myself for not remembering to look them up the last time I saw them. This particular flight, I happened to be running late, and was busy running from one end of the airport to the other trying to get through security. And once again I didn't look into it any further. I remember wanting to look up Porter on my phone but not having time. I made my flight, by the way, but I was sweating by the time I got to the gate, and I think I snuck in about four minutes before the door to the jetway closed.

Fast forward a few more months, and I'm in the airport with one of my co-workers, and we're talking about something work-related as we stroll by the Porter ticketing counter. Immediately, my internal alarms are sounding once again. PORTER. MUST FIND OUT MORE ABOUT PORTER. But, as luck would have it, my conversation about some video script or some client meeting continued. My focus soon returned to work, and Porter slipped out of my mind once again.

Strangely, my urge to fly Porter Airlines only grew and grew. The next time I went by the Porter counter, I had a little daydream about just walking up and asking the man behind the desk for a ticket. Mind you, I have never just flown anywhere in my life on a whim, and at this point, I still didn't even know where Porter flew, but I was seriously contemplating this possibility from well inside Daydream Land. In this specific case, I had a carry on and a personal item, so my hands were not free to check my phone and finally get the scoop on Porter. I made a pact with myself: As soon as I got on the plane, and before they made us shut off our phones, I was going to look up Porter Airlines once and for all!

And so I did!

Except that by the time I reached my seat on the plane, my phone was dead. I slumped down in my chair and just stared at my phone. I could see my dejected reflection staring back at me from the screen. I did a quick re-assessment of the situation. For over a year, I had been maintaining this completely nonsensical infatuation with an airline—an airline!—but somehow, had lacked the ability to do anything about it. I was either too busy, too forgetful, or just too inept to keep my phone charged to allow myself to end my own misery and finally find out about Porter. I stared into my phone's blank screen, closed my eyes and went to sleep.

Earlier this year, I flew on Spirit Airlines. Another somewhat obscure airline. This of course brought memories of Porter rushing into my head. I was already in my seat, no distractions to slow me down, my phone was charged. I was going to do it. I was going to Google Porter Airlines, this was going to be the end of it!

"So, do you live in Chicago?" The voice from next to me startled me as I started to open a new browser window on my phone.

I looked up, and the middle-aged man next to me was looking at me, as if he expected an answer.

Not wanting to be rude, I put my phone back in my pocket and informed the man that I used to live in Chicago and was going to visit family.

Wouldn't you know it! He used to live in Chicago, too. He was an actor, and he also taught acting and produced shows at a community theater. He'd even worked on the production crew for the movie "Blue Streak"! Yes, that "Blue Streak," the 1999 classic with Martin Lawrence. Martin Lawrence had made more than $10 million on that film, and this guy had gotten to drive him around. Apparently Martin Lawrence wasn't even that grateful to the crew. Can you imagine that? This guy also liked golf, especially Phil Mickelson. They were both lefties; it helped forge a bond between them. He always rooted for Phil. Always. But, he didn't believe in expensive golf equipment. Expensive drivers were a terrible waste of money. Secondhand was the only way to go. He also had lived in D.C. for a time. And New York. New York was a good city. But Chicago was, too...

Let's just say I didn't get to look up Porter Airlines before the flight attendant informed passengers that it was time to power down all electronic devices...

The plane landed after 11 p.m. I'm pretty sure my ears were sweating, and I was so exhausted I didn't remember to look up Porter when I was able to turn my phone on again. Besides, I was at O'Hare this time. There would be no Porter counter to remind me to finish my pursuit for the Holy Grail of airline knowledge.

On my return flight back to Nashville—this time back in the friendly confines of Chicago Midway—I was again running a little late, but after I entered the ticketing concourse, I sensed great-ness in the air. Even without seeing the Porter counter, my mind was ready. My phone was charged. I had but one carry-on, and an ever important free hand for Googling.

I would wait to get through security so as not to drop my phone. The security line was nearly deserted. All signs still pointed to victory.

Through security I hurried my way to my gate. I arrived at the gate to find that the B boarding group was in process of boarding. How could this be? How was I so late? I had breezed through security. I looked up again at the monitor. I was at the wrong gate. This flight was going to Kansas City, not Nashville. No!

I readjusted my bag on my shoulder and started what I like to call the "brisk hurried, but don't look at me walk" back through the terminal to the correct gate. This is a somewhat panicked walk, but not so much so that you make a complete scene. It's somewhere between the "business man on a mission" and "my wife's in labor," on the scale of walking speeds. In fact, "my wife's in labor" probably isn't even a walk at all. That one's probably better described as "careening through the walkway with little regard for other humans."

Either way, I needed to get to my new gate—and fast.

I got there, and there were still people in the waiting area. Thank you, thank you.

I had to use the restroom, but that would be fine, because there was still time. I came back from the restroom and saw that Boarding Group A was starting to board. That was me. I stood in line to board, and finally had an opportunity to pull my phone back out. Porter would be mine!

'Welcome to Boingo Airport Wi-Fi. Please sign in to continue!'

No! No! No!

I'm not going to pay for Wi-Fi, I'll use my phone signal to get to the Internet. I went into settings, and made a fatal error. I meant to turn Wi-Fi off, but in my haste, I turned the phone into Airplane Mode. Airplane Mode not only means no Wi-Fi, it also means no phone carrier signal either. As I was committing this error, I was also making my way onto the plane. Briefly, I paused to take my seat, a middle seat between an older gentleman, and a woman who looked to be about my mom's age.

I sat, put my book in the seat back pocket, and got my phone out. I wanted to be quick so that I would have time to use the phone before they closed the doors. I opened up Google, and entered my query. Simple, straight forward, it simply said, Porter Airlines.

At the same moment, the woman to my left said, "Hello." Normally, I would have waited a second just to see the Google result on the screen pop up, but I was a little taken aback that she'd be talking to me so soon into the flight process. Usually people let you get settled a little before they start talking to you.

That was okay in my mind, though. My phone was already loading my search query, no matter when I looked at it, even if it was later, after I had turned my phone off and back on after takeoff, I'd be fine. The screen would be loaded on my phone, and I'd be able to access the first page of a Google results page whether I was online or not!

The first page of Google would be plenty to quench my thirst for Porter information. I was sure it would tell me where the company was based, how old it was, maybe how many airplanes they had...

So, I started talking to the lady next to me. She was from Charlotte and going to Nashville to have a fun weekend with her friend. He sons were grown. She did HR for a large hair salon in Charlotte, and her husband worked in the beverage industry. During this time, I turned my phone off, as the flight attendant came by to remind everyone to do so. Again, I wasn't worried, the information would be there when I powered back on once were at cruising height.

I heard a little bit more about the life of the HR lady from Charlotte, and then I pulled out my book and did some reading. I got pretty involved with my book, and didn't even notice the pilot tell the plane that electronics were again allowed. The woman pulled out her IPad and started to play Candy Crush. Despite the game's immense popularity, I'd never seen it in person. I had no idea what it looked like, how to play, or what the point of the game even was. So, naturally, I had to ask the woman. For the next twenty minutes or so, she showed me Candy Crush—how to play, some of the strategy, and some of the difficult things about passing the level she was currently on. It wasn't hard to see how people get addicted to games like Candy Crush. After about twenty five minutes of that, I was ready to end this caper and find out about Porter.

I turned my phone back on, and immediately realized my mistake. A window was on the screen telling me that my original browser window had never loaded. The server couldn't be reached, and the page was blank.

How was this possible? I had specifically done this so that the page would still be there when I turned the phone back on. There were other browser windows with pages I had landed on that I was still able to read, why was this one different?

And then I realized it. I went to my phone settings to find that Airplane Mode had already been on. I had turned it on prior to looking up Porter, and thus it had never loaded in the first place.

I just smiled. Are you kidding me, I thought.

Upon landing, I had emails and phone calls waiting for me, and attended to them. Before I knew it, I was on the shuttle back to the economy parking lot, and within minutes I was back at home, still on the line with work.

As had been my theme, I forgot about Porter once I was out of the air travel world, and weeks passed again before thinking about it.

Until today!

I was at home, and out of nowhere, Porter Airlines came into my head. I was at home, and nothing stood in my way between the elusive knowledge. My Internet was in full working order. Nothing could stop me.

I started typing into Google on my phone, P-o-r-t-e-r ....

Usually by this time, the word or phrase you're trying to look up is starting to show up on the list of options in the Google box... Porter ridge, porter paints, Porter Road Butcher of all things, nothing about Porter Airlines.

Finally I entered an A, and Porter Airlines came up.

Here it was. This was it...

The first listing was their own page, and then some news items, and then finally, Wikipedia.

"Porter Airlines is a regional airline headquartered in Billy Bishop Toronto City Airport."

What? Porter was a Canadian regional airline? Headquartered in Toronto? They were founded in 2006? And as of today, had only 26 airplanes? Twenty-six!

My mind coughed, as my brain tried to process this information. Over the course of two years, I was secretly consumed by Porter Airlines. I was so embarrassed about this, I told nary a soul—and as you're finding out, I'll pretty much tell anyone anything...

All of this for a Canadian Regional Airline. UN. REAL.

I leaned my head against the cabinet in my kitchen and nearly started to cry. Then it hit me.

Who's up for a trip to Nova Scotia?

Learn Like a Kid

In what may have been the first occurrence in recent world history, I—a childless, nieceless, nephewless, young cousinless, non-babysitting twentysomething not under the influence of some illegal substance—watched "Sesame Street" today. And not only did I watch "Sesame Street," I watched "Sesame Street OnDemand." It was amazing.

I did it because I wanted to see how children learn. Or, at the very least, how the creators of "Sesame Street" think they learn. I trust them, after all, I think they're on season 44 of their show. I was watching episode 4,000-something. In this episode Telly and Elmo were teaming up to help Lil Bo Peep find her missing cow.

The cow-seeking duo was illustrating the word of the day, which was "pair."

As the two furry puppets searched for the missing bovine, they came across the tracks of other animals that weren't cows. Each interaction with the wrong track became a teachable moment to teach the viewers (I almost said "kids," but then realized I was watching, and a lot of parents were, too!) about each animal, about problem solving skills, and about the positive attitude necessary to keep searching for answers after the first clue doesn't result positively.

After identifying chicken tracks, raccoon tracks, and moose tracks, the team was about to give up, but then Elmo makes a few key inferences about some of the lessons they'd been learning, and urges the team to keep trying!

Of course, it is a little bit corny. Give the writers a break, they're targeting four year olds!

But I think if there's one thing that the folks at PBS have figured out is that anything they write should enhance the exuberance of a child to learn.

Think about how children learn. It's breathtaking.

If you are working with a two year old, and you tell the two year old to point to the picture of an apple, watch how excitedly they do it. And then, if praised, watch the outward signs of joy they display simply for being able to correctly identify a piece of fruit. There is no apple. They don't even get to eat the apple, and yet, just being able to know the answer is enough to bring them to unbelievable levels of joy. Kids will do this over and over. They will watch the same video clips over and over. And they love it every time! Ask any parent of a toddler how many times their child has watched the same video. Without fail, the number will be north of fifty.

And yet, think about the bad habits adults fall into.

"Jim, point at an apple."

"No."

"Come on Jim, point at an apple."

"Why should I?"

"Just because, maybe even for no reason, just point at an apple."

"What's in it for me? Do I get an apple if I do? Better yet, do I get twenty bucks if I do?"

"No Jim, just—"

Jim points at the apple, but immediately says, "Okay, what was that for? Why did I have to point at the apple?"

Okay, so this is another corny example, but somewhere amidst the human experience, the innocence of childhood is lost. The zeal for life. The zest for learning.

That's sad.

As I sat watching "Sesame Street," I could have been watching baseball, or football, or "The Walking Dead." But instead, I was watching Elmo and Telly look for Lil Bo Peep's cow. A happy looking lady named Sarah Jessica helped explain what a pair was, and there wasn't a cynical word to be said.

Did the kids know that Sarah Jessica was Sarah Jessica Parker from "Sex and the City"? Of course not. Did they care? Of course not. Did they learn what a pair was? Of course they did.

I turned off my corny meter. I turned off my lame barometer. I turned off what society has told me detect in "adult" situations. And it was awesome.

Now...I'm not sure I could watch all 54 minutes of the show—I watched twenty—nor do I think I could watch that episode 46 times over the course of 39 days...But for the time it would take to watch a mindless sitcom (which I also love), I was able to embrace my inner child. I had a smile on my face the entire time, and am smiling ear to ear now as I write this.

There's a reason Elmo in an international superstar. If you can't laugh at that little dude, you really need to check yourself.

Want some more good news?

"Sesame Street" is on every weekday at 10 a.m. Set your DVR. I promise, it's worth it!

They're Famous
to Somebody

I do a fair amount of driving in cities other than my home city. Having moved in the last couple of years, I've gotten a chance to learn my way around Nashville, and am pretty familiar with its streets. It took a while, but after 25+ years in Chicago, I finally feel like I know Nashville as well as my old home town.

If you spend enough time driving in any large city, you start to see a lot of the same street names. You've got your Washingtons and your Jeffersons, your Unions and your Church Streets. It seems like every other city has a Martin Luther King Drive, and somewhere there's a State and a Main. There's a certain level of familiarity that you can gain from seeing these names, even if you're in Louisville for the first time. Sure, it may be a little different this time around, but at least when you're driving and you see MLK Boulevard, you don't have to think twice about it. You know it's a main street, and you can easily figure that you'll find your way somewhere decently important if you stay on it.

After the most common names come the regionally important names. The Nashville area, for example, has all sort of street names that have to do with Andrew Jackson. In every other city, the war hero turned president may have Jackson Street, but in Tennessee, they've taken it a bit further. Old Hickory Boulevard runs all over Nashville, Donelson Pike is the namesake of his wife, Rachel Donelson, and Hermitage Avenue is named after his estate, The Hermitage. Things like this are pretty cool, as well; they give you a sense of local history as you drive around, and add a level of culture to the overall experiences of everyday life.

An even different level of street name coolness comes with themed names. I love to drive through smaller neighborhoods and try to identify the theme. It's often not very hard, but it's still fun to do. Trees, rivers and famous horses seem to be developers' favorites. And of course who could forget the golf course community? Just try and go to a golf course community without a Fairway Drive. I dare you to find one!

My favorite street names may be the most unassuming of all. Most days I drive by Isabella Lane on my way by a shopping center in Smyrna. Who is Isabella? Well, as we learned, in my rant about Columbus Day sales earlier on in this book, she was the Queen of Spain at the time of Columbus. There is, of course, Isabella Rossellini, the actress who is the daughter of Ingrid Bergman and once married Martin Scorsese. Somehow it seems unlikely that either of these Isabellas is being memorialized in a shopping center in Tennessee. More likely, it's the daughter, wife or mother of the developer, and I think that's awesome.

In the little town of Bethany, Missouri, there's a street called Lorraine Avenue. My great grandfather built his house on a new street in the town, and as the contractor who oversaw the concrete being poured for the street, the town let him name it. Lorraine Avenue memorializes his daughter – my grandmother – who died of polio the year before the house was completed. That might have something to do with my love for the street names we all don't know.

Or maybe it's because of Debbie Court, which stands about a quarter mile from where I grew up in Naperville, Illinois. When I was young, there was an old farmer who lived down the street from us. His name was Elmer, and he'd lived in town before there was much of a town. The city of Naperville has been annexing land for quite some time, and Elmer was one of the last farmers left with some land on 87th Street (Author's Note: Numbered streets do not get their own write up in this section. I love numbers, and I love streets, but numbered streets are just so unoriginal. I understand their place for making logical sense out of navigation, but there's really nothing fun about Sixth Street following Fifth.).

As a kid my brother and I used to ride our bikes to the library with my mom. On the way, we would have to pass Elmer's house.

He was super old and wore overalls. He didn't have much hair, and he only had one hand. This was a pretty intimidating combo to a kid, and I remember being kind of creeped out to ride by Elmer's place. But every time we went by, my mom would call out, "There's Elmer's house!"

Of course, the twerps that my brother and I could be at times, we called back, "We know, Moooom!" Every time. Until one day we saw a developer's sign in the yard at Elmer's house and stopped. Elmer came over and talked to my mom for a bit and explained that someone finally gave him an offer he couldn't refuse. He was going to keep his house on the corner, but he was going to sell his land behind it to be developed. He'd long since farmed anything on the property. It was just a matter of time before he was rewarded for his patience and cashed in on his land. A cul-de-sac went up behind his house, and before the first driveway foundations were even poured, a sign that read "Debbie Court" sprang up like a weed in Elmer's fields. Debbie was Elmer's daughter, or granddaughter, I can't remember which. It doesn't matter.

What does matter is that Elmer knows, and his family knew, too. They've all since passed on now, relics from an earlier time. The traffic that whizzes by on Naper Boulevard probably rarely thinks of Elmer. Even fewer still know the significance of the Debbie in Debbie Court. I barely do. I can't remember who she is exactly, but that doesn't stop me from thinking about her, and about Elmer every time I drive by.

For every Rosa Parks, Martin Luther King, or George Washington Street, there's even more Isabellas, Lorraines and Debbie Courts out there. They might not have had as formal a role in shaping the United States as those other luminaries, but don't try and tell that to their fathers...

Tomorrow you'll drive by a street with a "nobody" name. Except the truth is, they're all famous to somebody.

You Don't Know
Until You Know

About ten years ago or so, a guy name Ken Jennings went on a 74-episode run on the TV show "Jeopardy." He won more than $2 million, and quite possibly he may be the most popular Mormon computer scientist of all time. I remember watching Jennings play and thinking, "What doesn't this guy know?"

Eventually he got beat on Jeopardy, and along the way there were questions he didn't know, but in general, it just seemed like he knew everything. I mean, even to be able to come up with guesses that correctly answered so many questions is remarkable to think about.

I like "Jeopardy," and like to think I'm decent at it. If I get about three to five questions right every round, I am pretty pleased with myself. Of course, this is child's play for most contestants, and I know the level of their knowledge exponentially far trumps mine.

At the time Jennings was making his run on "Jeopardy," I think I was either a senior in high school, or possibly a freshman in college. I had come from a great upbringing, I had worked at a very prestigious golf course for five years, had traveled a bit, and generally thought of myself as all kids of this age did: I knew pretty much everything about everything. I had a car, I had finally figured out how all the major highways in Chicagoland were interconnected, and I had just joined a credit union. As a one-time winner of the "Find all 50 State License Plates on One Road Trip" game, I was about as worldly as anyone would ever need to be. In my own mind at least.

I guess that's why it's good to go to college and continue to expose yourself to new things. I've learned since then that it's impossible to know everything, but I had no idea how much I didn't know.

I remember sitting in computer science class my freshman year of college, and it was as if Marsha Woodbury was speaking some sort of language that couldn't possibly be real. The silly part was it was basic HTML.

I had some kids on my floor that were talking about circuits for their electrical engineering class. I knew the word "engineering," but truthfully, I remember coming back to my college dorm room, and Googling, "What is engineering?"

This may seem preposterous, but I honestly didn't know what engineering was. I later found out that my grandpa was an efficiency engineer, but as a kid, you don't necessarily learn those things. Or, if you did know them, they were explained to you in such a way that you might not realize what was being described to you is actually engineering.

I'm very proud of the upbringing I had. My dad is a car salesman, and for most of my life my mom was a stay-at-home mom. I always felt like I was well-informed. I went to great schools growing up and did pretty well. Maybe if my dad had been a consultant or a different kind of salesperson, I'd have known those things. But he wasn't, and I didn't.

As I continued to grow in college, more and more things like this came up. The old adage about learning more outside the classroom in college was definitely true.

It's not exactly the same thing as learning what engineering is, but I still remember the first time I saw someone do cocaine. It was kind of one of those moments where things got quiet in my head, and I thought, "Well, I guess that was what it looks like when someone does cocaine..." It was deeply disturbing, but at the same time, one of those things you can't really know about until you know about it.

I guess the most interesting, and most unexpected part of my life is the fact that I'm still having those moments nearly every day where I find things that are still so new, and so mind boggling, I can't even believe it sometimes.

We have a client at work who makes industrial boiler cleaning equipment. Inside those boilers are tubes that have to be cleaned. This process keeps the boiler clean, running efficiently, and safe. Our client makes automated and partially automated systems that help do this tube rolling and cleaning process more quickly.

Our client has a team of engineers that write software for their machines that allows their tools to automatically sense and then produce movements at exact levels of torque pressure.

If those last two paragraphs don't make sense to you, don't worry, you're not alone. I remember when we first picked up this company as a client, I was so uninformed about what they did, I actually had to look up what an industrial boiler looked like.

I once had an internship where the company I was working for made particulate monitors to put on smokestacks. I barely knew what the EPA was, let alone how you'd go about making one of these monitors. I remember going through orientation at this company, and literally feeling like I was the most underqualified human in the history of internships.

I recently heard about someone throwing a Gender Reveal Party. Obviously this isn't a hard concept to grasp, but having never had someone close to me go through that process, I had no idea that was a type of party that people had.

Sometimes things like these manifest themselves in the form of obscure knowledge. That ridged area of your upper lip below your nose, that's called a Philtrum. The snap or button on the top of a baseball cap, that's called a squatchee. The seed of a pomegranate, that's called an aril.

These things are all completely random, and definitely not things I knew before someone told me, but it doesn't make them less cool.

I was talking to a guy who had a job at a logistics company the other day. His job was to fulfill the orders for forks and knives and spoons from a distribution center to every KFC in the country.

Think about that. Somewhere in the middle of Wyoming (Riverton, Wyoming, on North Federal Boulevard, if you must know) there is a KFC that needs forks, and there's a guy in Tennessee that makes sure that happens.

As you read this, maybe you're saying to yourself, "Well Matt, welcome to life. Life is all about learning new things and being amazed by them." Well in that case, cool. I like this thing called life. Even if there's a whole lot more about it that I have to learn...

Carving a Pumpkin

I'm a firm believer in trying your best no matter what. I also think that until you've tried something, you shouldn't write yourself off as being unable to do it. Buuuuut, in a similar vein of not trying to teach every pig to fly, I probably shouldn't legally be allowed to try to carve a pumpkin. Arts and crafts plus sharp cutting utensils has never been a winning equation for me. I very nearly cut off part of my finger trying to prune a hydrangea bush one time...

So of course, what did I try and do today?

Carve a pumpkin, naturally.

Well, to be fair, there was a lot more that happened even before I got to the carving part.

I went to the farm stand and began my search for the perfect Jack-O-Lantern. Mind you, had I read the "Helpful Pumpkin Carving Tips" article that I would look at a few hours later, I would have known that larger pumpkins are actually easier to carve... So instead I bought a nice medium-sized, sharply curving pumpkin. It had a nice stem, a feature I was very proud of. I wanted to be able to very easily pull the lid off the pumpkin when I was done.

I paid the friendly kid at the farm stand my six dollars—what a steal, I thought!—and put the pumpkin in the front seat of my car to drive home.

Not one stoplight later, the pumpkin (let's call him Jack, so I don't have to keep writing out "the pumpkin") rolled over, and crack went the stem. The glorious lid handle that I had worked so hard to find was now hanging by a thread. I was crushed. Somehow, this process didn't seem to be off to a good start. I wasn't even home yet, and I'd almost broke Jack...

Upon arriving home, I carefully picked Jack up around his belly and cradled him inside. He was my wounded little duckling now (Author's Note: I'm not sure why Jack looked like a Jack and not a Jackie. Maybe I'm sexist, but most pumpkins just do not look very feminine.).

I cleared off my kitchen table, and began tearing out pages of an old magazine to protect the table from getting pumpkin guts all over as I carved. After the table was covered, I went about the task of selecting a knife to turn old Jack into something awesome...

I tried to think back to the years as a child that my dad had done this. If only I wasn't always watching football. Which knife did he use? I went over to my knife block—the same one my parents had growing up—and peered in. For some strange reason, I chose a large butcher knife, the same one my mom had used most of my life to cut watermelon. I figured, watermelon and pumpkins are similar sizes, how wrong could I be?

Very wrong, but we'll come back to that later.

Now that I had my knife picked out, I had to figure out a way to draw a circle around the top of Jack, to cut out his lid. Notice I said figure out how to draw a circle? This process took me about four minutes. As I was contemplating this move, I looked at the clock. I don't remember the time, but I distinctly remember wondering if I'd finish before Halloween was over? Right now, I was going with over...

With my circle drawn, I soon learned what most of you figured out a few minutes ago: Cutting a circle of a three-inch radius with a knife featuring a three-inch wide blade was not easy. Of course I had bought the smaller, thick-walled pumpkin, so I really had to dig the knife in pretty far to get through the outer wall. Imagine trying to cut a nice circle with a ruler...It didn't go well. Let's just say this took a while, and move on, shall we?

During this process, I started "old-man breathing." Old-man breathing is what old men inexplicably do while working very hard to complete very easy tasks. I finished cutting the lid off Jack, and I was sweating and breathing heavily. I held the lid by its top, careful not knock off the rest of the stem. I was feeling like I was as good as done, feeling like I'd run about two miles, and also feeling quite silly.

Why did I feel like I was marathon training? I was carving a pumpkin. And better yet, I hadn't even really carved the pumpkin yet. I had cut a hole in the top...I looked at the clock again. Sigh.

Focused again, I decided to cut the layer of pumpkin skin and seeds off the bottom side of Jack's lid. I did this without issue. Win! But then, I picked it up. Wow. Pumpkin guts felt weird. Gooey. Gross. Ugh. Why did I try this again? I threw them into the garbage and set to dig out the rest of Jack's guts.

I chose an old silver slotted spoon for the excavation. I was pretty good at this. I remember as a kid my mom would occasionally toast the pumpkin seeds we harvested from our Jack-O-Lanterns, but as I scooped the seeds out of Jack, they didn't look very good. I felt bad, but I didn't save them.

It was at this time that I realized I had done all the easy stuff; it was actually time to carve. I went online and searched for "How to Carve a Pumpkin?" I was one of those people that type out an entire question in Google like it's Ask Jeeves from 1998. But, on this topic, that's about all I was good for.

The pumpkin carving site talked about how you must cut your lid at a 45 degree angle so that once removed it wouldn't fall back into the hole you'd just cut...

Oh no. Geometry? I hadn't even considered the angle at which I was cutting the lid... I was just trying not to cut my thumb off while making square cuts in the shape of a circle!

I picked up the lid and placed it on Jack's head.

Thankfully, it fit. I was an hour into this process, and the last thing I wanted was for the lid to be ruined and my project to be over before it started...

The helpful tips then said to draw out your design on paper, and then transfer it to the pumpkin when you were satisfied with what you had drawn. It suggested doing classic shapes if you were a beginner, and not trying anything too complicated if this was your first carve.

I pulled out a yellow sheet of legal pad paper, and drew three triangles for the eyes and nose. Doesn't get much more basic than that!

Excited, I drew the triangles on Jack's sort-of-soon-to-be face. I kind of missed the center... Luckily, I was using non-permanent marker and was able to wipe off my poorly drawn shapes with a wet rag. Although, now Jack was all wet, and marker wouldn't stick to him.... So, I had to go get a towel and dry him off. Here I was swaddling a pumpkin that I was now more than an hour into carving, and I still only had a lid to show for my efforts...Well, a lid and a piece of paper with three triangles on it. If that counts for anything.

I got Jack all dry and started again. Using a much smaller knife this time, I made a grand discovery: If you just cut in straight lines, you don't even need a marker to simply cut a triangle out of a pumpkin. Imagine that. I dug the much more manageable knife into Jack's face, and within seconds I had an eye!

I stood back looking at what I'd just done. I looked at Jack so proudly, you would have thought he just earned a Master's degree! What a feeling. I made a Jack-O-Lantern eye! I then made another. And then a nose. Three triangles. Not fancy. Not symmetrical, but triangles! I felt like Michelangelo.

And then came time to try the mouth. This was going to be a tough one. What do Jack-O-Lantern mouths look like again? Again, I searched the Internet, this time for images.

I saw what others had done. A lot of diagonal lines. Looked easy enough. So, I went to my legal pad. Somehow I drew a crescent shaped half-moon. I stared at it in disbelief. I knew I was bad at drawing, but how does one try to draw an accordion style array of diagonal lines and end up with a half-moon? I tried again. The result looked like a hot dog that someone took an awkward bite out of...Ugh. This was not going well. Could I just draw one big triangle and cut that out?

I decided I'd just forgo the legal pad and just draw something on Jack. Winging it, I drew what kind of looked like a cartoon whale. Sweet, I thought, that's way better than if I would have tried to draw a whale...

But I didn't need a whale, I needed a crooked-toothed smile!

Finally, I had an idea worthy of my Tennessee residence! Crooked teeth? How about no teeth??

And with that, I cut a small rectangular slit that spanned from one end of Jack's face to the other. It was perfect. I squealed with delight! I didn't just feel like Michelangelo, I was Michelangelo. I picked up Jack and rocked him in my arms like a little baby. I had never felt so connected to a piece of fruit in my life. It was amazing. Jack was like family now!

I placed a small candle inside of him, lit it, put his lid on, and stood back to admire my masterpiece. Staring back at me was the simplest, most generic Jack-O-Lantern in the history of mankind. And, he didn't even have teeth. But you know what? I made him. I had done it. I had conquered an art and craft!

It sounds silly, but I really did feel so good at that moment. Arts, crafts and really anything that is done with the hands instead of the mind is never something that has come easy to me. I can't draw, I don't build, I don't fix, I don't sculpt. If you ask my dad and brother, I can't even screwdriver...

But on this night, I cut, and I carved, and I crafted. I sat in the dark in my apartment and just watched Jack's toothless, indifferent expression illuminate the room, and I smiled. I smiled really big. It was definitely a smile I couldn't have carved, nor was it one that I ever could have imagined. But here it was, and boy, did it feel good.

Happy Halloween, Bob Dole

I'm not much for celebrity worship. The way I see it, celebrities probably have it pretty similar to how I have it. The roots of their problems are probably like mine, too. Sure, they probably go about solving their problems differently, with different means, and different social expectations. But in the end, we're all pretty much the same. We're people, trying to navigate our way through life.

Except on Halloween.

How must it feel to Rhianna or Justin Bieber and to have people dress up as you?

Or how must it feel to be Michelle Obama and have people dress up in a classy manner to mimic your style... and then see the second half of a costumed duo wearing a silly caricature of your husband's face in the form of a mask?

I'm sure all of these people have much better things to do than worry about how they are being portrayed on Halloween, but still...

Justin Timberlake may be the only celebrity completely immune to Halloween ridicule. As if he needed to prove in any more ways that he's just better than everyone else at everything, JT owns Halloween, too.

If someone were to be a Mousketeer from the old Mickey Mouse Club, JT could be like, "Yeah, I was one of those... You want to fight about it?"

For a while there in the 1990s, groups of people actually dressed up as N'SYNC for Halloween, and while it may not have been the thing they're most proud of now, you can assure yourself that they weren't lacking any female attention that night...

And just in case there may have been some lingering feelings from what happened in the 1990s, Timberlake got some help from his buddy Andy Samberg on "Saturday Night Live" in 2006 to get rid of those. In the skit, JT was just trying to get his girl what she really wanted for Christmas... And wouldn't you know it, it became one of the most well-remembered inspirations for a Halloween costume in recent memory. After something like that, the guy has Halloween street cred for at least two more decades.

But not everyone can be as cool as Justin Timberlake.

In 1996, Bob Dole ran for president, and as is usually the case, presidential masks were a big hit that year. I'm sure he was ready for it, but in other ways I'm sure it must have shocked him to see his face on a mask like that. Bob Dole was born in Russell, Kansas, in 1923. Do you think he ever thought in a million years that one day he'd have teenagers wandering around college towns with his likeness strapped to their face?

It's one thing to have something like that happen after the person has died—like Marilyn Monroe—but to have it take place while you are living must be kind of odd.

It must be even stranger now for Bob Dole to look back on it. Bob Dole recently celebrated Bob Dole's 90th Halloween, and for the first 72, he probably enjoyed it just like everyone else would. Then, on his 73rd, things got crazy, as to be expected when you run for president. But, I'd be willing to bet there haven't been too many Bob Dole costumes in the Halloweens since 1996. I wonder how he views Halloween now? I really do... I wonder if he hands out candy thinking about all of the little kids whose parents were him for Halloween in 1996?

"Oh, that's cute there little kid, you're a lady bug! Back before you were born, your dad was me for Halloween, what do you think about that?" Talk about scaring a kid for life...

Do you think any of Bob Dole's friends bought up a bunch of the masks and still pull them out once in a while? Maybe Bob himself wears one around the house to give Elizabeth a scare every once in a while? If he's around next year, I can only hope Bob goes as himself for Halloween.

"Who are you this year, Bob?"
"Well, you know, Bob Dole is Bob Dole for Halloween."
Of course he is...

Pungent Rumors

I love going to the grocery store. I love the smells. I love watching people push their carts, wrangle with their coupons, or put together a nice dinner. It's always fun to go around Thanksgiving; with one quick glance in the cart, and you can see all the fixins' coming together for a big family meal. The checkout line is even more fun. In the most non-nosey manner I can muster, I like to just see what people buy – not because I really care but because it's just interesting note. Moms with kids buy a lot of lunch snacks and breakfast food. Middle-aged single men do not.

In fact, if there was ever to be a "Divorced Male" persona to create at the grocery store, that guy would buy a Jack's Pizza, a six pack of relatively cheap domestic beer, one package of pre-cooked bacon, and a bag of plain Ruffles potato chips. Captain Cholesterol tends to do this late at night, and always goes to the self-checkout line. It's like clockwork. Go to a grocery store at 8:45 p.m. on a Wednesday, and stay there for a half hour. You'll see this guy. He's usually wearing a white undershirt and slacks. I would know. I go to the grocery store a lot (Author's Note: Dear Lord, I apologize in advance for pointing this out. I've started to repent right now in hope that this is never the man I become.).

I live by a Target that has a grocery store inside, and my love of grocery stores brings me there most days. I know Target isn't the best supermarket, but it's within walking distance of my house, and it's a good excuse to get out and go for a walk. Let's just say for a single person who has no other mouths to feed, I probably lead the league in yearly grocery store visits.

And yet, the other day at Target, something happened that had never happened at any other time during any other grocery store visit.

I'll set the scene for you. I walked over to Target to pick up bananas and some ranch dressing (No, I wasn't eating them together, that'd be gross.). It was about 8 p.m., and an unseasonable 65 degrees for an October night in Nashville. It was dark, and the Target parking lot was hopping with excitement.

I got a little spring in my step. Who knew what I might see tonight!?

Except it wasn't what I saw, it was what I smelled. As I approached the store, the distinct odor of what seemed like an army of skunks assaulted my poor nose. About two hundred yards from the store, my eyes began to tear up. Whoa, this was one of the worst smelling skunk attacks I'd smelled in a while.

I thought to myself, I can't wait to get inside; it was that bad.

Finally, I reached the doors and went inside. Except when I opened my nose and stopped breathing out of my mouth, it wasn't any better. For a second, I thought it was me, but then I saw other people in other parts of the store turning their noses up at the smell. Besides, I had showered that day!

As I moved through the store, I realized, I'd never been in a store that was so much under the influence of a skunk spray. It was kind of fun seeing people's reactions. The smell was unbearably bad, but it was so universally bad that it was like a wave was passing through the store. You could see people fifty feet ahead in a wide aisle as the smell made its way toward them. If I would have been standing there with anyone, I could have punched them in the side and been like, "3-2-1, now," and the smell would have hit them. It was like clockwork, and it had people coughing and stammering.

I was loving every second of it. I had a headache, the smell was so bad, but this was an all-time first. It seemed as though there might be a skunk in Target. It's amazing this had never happened before. I had once been in a furniture store where a bird was flying around, but that's about the extent of my animal interaction during shopping escapades.

I quickly picked up my bananas and ranch (Okay, now that really sounds like a flavor, and that flavor sounds awful.) and stepped out into the area of the store from where the strongest smell seemed to be coming.

In every direction, people were looking to the floor as if trying to spot a skunk. I was staring at the Halloween section, and people were stewing about. But there was no skunk.

I made my way to the register area, and all of the checkout associates were covering their noses, and mouths. Some of the younger ones were asking if there was a skunk in the store.

Really, a skunk in the store? This was the official rumor now. Patrons coming in from outside started paused by the front doors upon entering. The customer service manager was apologizing for the smell and assuring people there was no skunk. But it didn't matter.

I quickly paid for my two items and hurried to be on my way. My checkout person actually buried her nose in the front of her red shirt as she rang up my dressing...

As I made my way outside, a congregation was gathering, as they watched the people just inside not moving past the entrance.

Soon, the rumor had spread outside. "There's a skunk in the candy section!" someone yelled. Cars were stopping in the parking lot, people were rolling their windows down and asking each other how many skunks were inside?

I laughed and shook my head. This was unbelievable.

Right now, I was at the epicenter of a rumor mill.

How long would it be before animal control was called?

Or maybe the National Guard? Someone get on the phone with the governor...

I wanted to just stop everyone and tell them I was just looking at the candy aisle two minutes ago and there was no skunk.

But what fun would that be?

I said nothing, smiled, and walked home.

Slam Dunk!

O ver the last couple of weeks, I've been blessed with a new opportunity. Among all the other things I am in life, I can now add the title of "10- and 11-Year-Old Volunteer Basketball Coach" to my list.

A while back, my friend John heard about the possibility of the West Wilson (County) Basketball Association possibly needing volunteer coaches if any of their teams wound up without a parental volunteer. He asked me if that was the case if I'd be interested in helping him coach a team. I thought about it for about a half second and excitedly replied, "Yes!"

For far too long, and of no fault but my own, I'd been yearning to get involved in the community, and this was the perfect opportunity. Practices would be at night, and within ten minutes of my house. Games would be on weekends, and the overall time commitment necessary was perfect with my work schedule. Despite never being a sport at which I excelled growing up, basketball is a game that I have had some experience playing and is something that I truly enjoy. In addition, I'd refereed basketball for kids similar to this age while I worked for the YMCA in high school. So, I was familiar with the rules, the type of play I could expect, and the expectations of the kids and the parents at this level. And finally, I'd been playing a lot of pickup basketball at the park by my house lately, so my basketball skills themselves were sharper than usual, and my interest in the game was at a level it hadn't been in quite a while.

Going into the season, my biggest question mark rested with the kids. It had been a long time since I'd spent time with 10- and 11-year-olds, and that kind of had me anxious. The last time I spent much time with kids of that age, I'd been a 17-year-old high school kid. I was much closer to the kids' age, and also wasn't really in a position where I had to demonstrate much responsibility. Sure, as a referee I was in charge of running the games, but ultimately the coaches handled most of the discipline and kept the kids in order.

Over the last decade plus, I've definitely grown into an adult, but in many ways not a responsible one. Well, not in the context of overseeing kids at least. I am responsible for myself, for my work, for paying my bills, and for being a functioning member of society, but none of that is at all like being responsible for a child. Heck, I've been known to get nervous doing pet sitting. Coaching kids seemed much more demanding than walking and poop-coaxing. At the end of a few minutes pet sitting, you put the pet where you're supposed to, and you get to go home. As a coach, you can't exactly just lock a kid in a cage and wait for his mom to come pick him up...Thankfully this coaching assignment was only a few days a week, and the league wasn't anything more than the county league for elementary school kids.

Needless to say, I was still nervous for our first practice. Would kids listen to John and me? Would they be able to do the drills we planned for them? Would our team be any good? What would the parents say? A million questions ran through my head.

And with the first practice began my amazement. For ten and 11 year olds, I was shocked. They were so good! A few of our kids could dribble behind their backs and through their legs, and one of our first layup lines produced a streak of five baskets in a row! I'm not sure why I thought they wouldn't be good, but just how good they were was pretty awesome to see.

With each practice, the kids seemed to get better and better. John and I kept coming up with new drills, and the kids really seemed to understand them. Sure, some of them were pretty rough looking, but for kids of 10 and 11, that's to be expected.

What I most struggled with early on was the kids' names. As you may have gathered throughout this book, I like to think I have a very good memory. I can remember the smallest details about a lot of strange things, but for some reason the names of my new players kept escaping me. Luckily for me, we only had eight players on our team. So in theory, remembering names shouldn't have been a problem.

And yet for some reason I just couldn't get down the name of a small blond-haired boy. For some reason I kept calling him Austin. Maybe ten or twenty times over the course of a few practices, I called him Austin over and over. Until finally, John informed me that his name was indeed Nathan.

Nathan, eh? I felt so bad. I had looked Nathan in the eye at least ten times and flat out called him Austin. "Good job Austin, Way to go, Austin. You'll get it, Austin!" And all this time, Nathan didn't say anything to correct me. It just made me feel like such a goober. The West Wilson Basketball Association parents tend to watch their kids practice, so over in the stands Nathan's mother was probably sitting there listening to this new coach call her son "Austin."

Talk about a good first impression.

The next practice we had, I finally was able to remember that Nathan's name was in fact Nathan, and I felt much better. But, there was still part of me that hoped he hadn't been offended by the fact that his coach didn't know his name, and time and time again got it wrong. I was the kid in grade school that felt terrible being the fifth or sixth 'Matt' in my class, but at least everyone knew my name. How bad would I have felt if for some reason the teacher was calling me "Walt"?

Austin and Nathan at least end in the same sound, but if you do that Matt vs. Walt test, it's pretty much equally as bad. Every time I looked at Nathan, I tried so hard to remember what his name was, and each time, I'd think to myself, "Is it Austin or Nathan?" It was an excruciating process. Coaching? Easy peazy. Name remembering? Much harder! Who would have known?

Overall, I felt great about where the team was at, where John and I were at as coaches, and just the experience of having fun with the kids. The genuinely looked up to us. They listened as well as you could expect kids to listen, and they were very respectful. The only mark on my conscience was the Nathan/Austin issue.

And then, something amazing happened.

I was walking around JCPenney looking for a pair of pants. If you must know, I was looking for a specific pair of pants for my Halloween costume. I'm not sure why I went to Penneys; I never go to Penneys. But, on that night I did.

I was trying to find the men's section when all the sudden the rapid clatter of running footsteps came up behind me. Before I had a chance to realize what was happening, or even had time to turn around, a finger poked me in the lower back. I was about to turn around when a small figure jumped out in front of me and yelled a most fitting greeting, "Slam dunk!"

It was Au— Nathan! He was here, in the store, and he just ran down the aisle to say hi. I was so thrown off I didn't hardly know what to say.

Finally I mustered words. "Hey (not Austin) Nathan! How are you, buddy!"

Yes! I had done it. I was shocked, and in the half second I had to produce the right name I had been up to the challenge!

Nathan and I talked for about five seconds. He told me he might not be at practice on Saturday. I found out that he was excited for Halloween, and we went our separate ways. We high fived before he left.

I felt amazing. The player that I had felt the worst about had come up and wanted to say hello.

Now, I know that I overthink everything, and I know that kids don't take someone calling them the wrong name a few times as seriously as I had made it out in my head—at least not 10 year-old boys—but resolving the awkward feeling still felt amazing.

I've never felt that way before. I'm not a parent, I've never been a teacher before, and I'm not even an uncle. It's a completely different feeling to have someone seek you out like that just to say hello, to tap you on the back and then jump out in front of you.

I can't slam dunk a basketball, and I don't even know yet how good of coaches John and I will be. We haven't even played our first game yet. It's possible we might be terrible. There's a pretty good chance we'll have a disagreement with a referee or a parent, or maybe both. Kids may cry, and they may be frustrating. I'm okay with that. As far as I'm concerned, this experience has already been worth it.

Thanks to my new buddy Nathan, I've already had my Slam Dunk! moment.

The Immeasurable

To say that I love data, and measuring data would be the understatement of all time. If you let him, my dad will tell you a story of a three year-old up almost until midnight with a stopwatch watching bowling. Yes, bowling. I was timing, in seconds, how long it took the bowlers to hurl their bowling ball down the lane. Over and over, I'd start-stop-reset my stopwatch. I have no idea what I was trying to do, but I just wanted to know how long it took, and if some bowlers bowled faster than others. I wish I could say I had a spreadsheet of my data, but sadly I do not. Needless to say, data measurement is something that I've always loved. Even at three. Even if it was bowling on TV.

Today, my job involves trying to measure certain marketing activity, and a lot of my free time is spent analyzing box scores and other sports-related data. I'm a happy man when it comes to data and its measurement.

But the strange thing is I love the immeasurable innumerably more! And for everything I love about the Internet, its ability to make almost anything measurable takes the fun out of a lot of my immeasurable day dreaming.

It used to be that you could just make blanket inquiries about things you were wondering about, and you'd just have to wonder about them or try to figure them out. Now, you just use Google.

Driving through a small town and wondering, "Man I bet this town has only fifteen cars registered between all its residents..." And truthfully, this was always something you COULD have looked up, but if you were just driving through town, how would you have ever found the County Registrar? Well, Google knows where it is... And thanks to the Internet, you can find almost anything.

As you may have guessed, I find great pleasure in trying to

stump the Internet. A few months ago I typed a single vertical bar into Bing, and it produced zero results. The vertical bar is this symbol, used to separate pieces of content on the web. |Sadly, Google has 1.9 million results for this query. I guess I'll have to keep trying to find something Google doesn't at least have a guess about...

Even logic questions that companies use to test job candidates have answers on the Internet. You know, the old, 'How many quarters would it take to cover a football field two inches tall from end zone to end zone?" Someone from MIT has worked that out for you on eHow, and the answer is there in the time it takes you to enter your query into Google. How fun is that?

I try to think more abstractly. It's fall right now, and that means my dad is in his yearly battle with the leaves falling in his yard. The man is obsessed. If you talk to him on a Saturday night and ask what the coming Sunday has in store, he'll tell you he'll probably go to church in the morning, and then it'll be time to "battle the leaves." Battling the leaf literally means trying to displace every single leave from the grass in his yard. All of them. As in, not leaving any on the lawn.

By literally all, I do not mean figuratively all. He will blow them. He will rake them. He will vacuum them up. It doesn't matter if the tree above him still has 4,000 leaves that have yet to fall. For that day, the goal always is "no leaves." This insanity-producing exercise has been going on for years, and quite frankly, I don't get it. My dad's a pretty smart guy, but what the heck is the point of raking all these leaves when thousands more are going to fall? Or, better yet, the wind may blow, and God forbid some of those leaves you just raked might end up back on the lawn five minutes after you finish. And yes, you can wet the leaves down by hosing down the pile in the street with a hose. Trust me, I know about that one...

But hey, who am I to judge? I used to measure the time it took for a bowling ball to make it from one end of a lane to another. Everyone is entitled to their quirks. If it were me, I'd rake once when all the leaves were off the trees... But, his house, his rules.

The best thing that has come from this leaf-raking obsession is an immeasurable situation. My dad has lived in his house for thirty years, and my question is simple: How many leaves has he raked in 30 years? Take that Google! His trees were of different heights and ages at all times within the measurement period. There were different wind patterns each year, meaning that some years some of his leaves may have blown away and other foreign leaves may have found their way into his leaf piles...

Even if he had somehow managed to bag every leaf he ever raked, and then taken an average of how many bags per year he used, and how many leaves per bag he collected in each bag, we'd still have very shoddy data. I mean, an oak leaf and a birch leaf are very different in size and weight. Trying to weigh a bag and get an average number of leaves is nearly impossible unless you know the exact breakdown of what's in the bag. And even Mr. Leaf himself doesn't have that data. HOWEVER, I will admit, that this situation may be measurable if the leaf collector cataloged every leaf they collected over a 30-year span. When I meet that guy, I'll be sure it's not fall...

Okay, maybe we can get even more immeasurable. How about the average age of all fine point pen users? Think Google's got that one? And while you're at it Google, could you tell me how that average age compares to medium point pen users?

Personally, I think as people get older and they start to appreciate fine penmanship a little bit more, their natural tendency is to start to employ fine tipped pens. Throw in the possibility of a twinge of arthritis making it difficult to execute crisp handwriting strokes, and a fine-tip pen is almost a necessity to make legible characters. But, maybe I'm wrong? Maybe there is a whole generation of youngbloods out there that were raised on fine-point gel pens, and that's all they'll use. Maybe the medium point is for old people? Let's take a pen-using census!

But how?

I mean, even if every pen produced from 2014 on was mandated by international law to have fingerprint recognition software built into its outer coating that was then connected to a database that logged pen usage and attributed it to its user and updated a running log in that database, you'd still have issues.

What about all the people not in the fingerprint database? What about all the old pens that weren't outfitted with the new technology? How do you account for them? Or better yet, what about the people who wear gloves while they use a pen for the one and only time of that pen-person relationship? Like at the bank in the winter...Do you think I'm going to take my glove off just so I can make sure the pen usage database is updated? Psh. You better believe I'm not. If it means I can preserve the sanctity of the immeasurable, there's no way!

Think about how many novelty companies would be in serious legal trouble if someone could figure out statistically who was the World's Best Dad? Whoever that guy is would have a lot of coffee cups coming his way in a settlement!

When someone tells you they like ketchup more than anyone in the world, it's probably for the best that you can't actually test for this. Ketchup is gross, after all. I can't imagine trying to come up with some test to quantify "Katchup Love," and then having to round up all of the world's ketchup eaters and watch them guzzle down the goopy stuff. Sorry Google, this one isn't going to happen either.

As a pregnant woman in Philadelphia is experiencing morning sickness for the sixth day in a row, it's probably best not to tell her exactly how many other morning sicknesses have been experienced over the course of history by other pregnant women across the world. It's best you just leave her alone. There's no statistic in the world worth sharing in that situation.

That is unless you can find the 10 millionth sugar cookie ever made, and give that to her a few years later. But, then again, how would you ever know? Cookies have been made for years. Who was keeping count? Maybe some czar of the grocery store industry knows exactly how many cookies have been sold since the beginning of record keeping, but how can he know how many cookies my grandma made? Or your Great Aunt Edna?

The immeasurables are the best because they're the things in life that you're not supposed to keep track of. Leaves on a lawn are meant to be put in piles for kids to jump in, for dogs to chase in the wind, or for artists to draw.

The greatest thing about a pen is that its ink can say whatever its ink says, regardless of who wrote it, or how old they were.

When you see a little boy enjoying ketchup on his chicken nuggets, it doesn't matter if someone else somewhere loves ketchup more than he does. For that moment in time, the love that he has for ketchup is all that matters.

Whether that pregnant cookie is the 10 millionth, or the 11,302,392nd, it comes at exactly the right time, every time.

In our data-driven world where every number means something, where every occurrence is a challenge to prove something else, it's nice to find those situations that defy measurement. Those situations where life is simply too vast to be reined in by the logic of the numerical systems created to bring it order.

You keep after those leaves, Pops. I'll be smiling for the upteenth time...

Trust Your Dreams
to a Cartoon Hot Dog

As often as possible, I try to visit local restaurants. I'm no foodie, and I do enjoy a visit to Chili's or Red Robin from time to time, but there's something about going to a local, non-franchised restaurant that really appeals to me. Especially since moving to Nashville, I've tried to take advantage of sampling the local flavor. I figure I can go to an Applebee's in pretty much any town in America, may as well save those visits for when I'm in a roadside town with few other options.

I'm also not a big restaurant reality TV show watcher, but I've seen enough on those shows to know that running a restaurant is not easy; especially not a startup that competes with many of the "fast casual" franchise chains that dominate the current landscape of American dining options.

I think that's a big reason that my recent visit to Cori's Dog House had such a profound effect on me. Cori's Dog House is what you might be able to guess that it is: a hot dog restaurant. Located in the Nashville suburb of Mt. Juliet, Cori's may as well be the symbol of the American Dream.

Sean Sullivan owns Cori's, and according to his own website, used to love going to Woolworth's with his mother as a kid. He'd sit at the counter and gobble down two hot dogs every time he visited. The fond memories left such a mark on Sully that more than 30 years later, he opened a hot dog place of his own. To put the cherry on top of the sundae, he named his restaurant after his nine year-old daughter, Cori, and gave the restaurant a cartoon dog hot as a mascot.

Actually, Cori's gets even more storybook. The tables and chairs are ketchup and mustard red and yellow, and they have a

Wall of Fame for any person who is successfully able to eat all of Cori's roughly 40 varieties of hot dogs. And wouldn't you know it, each variety represents a different regional take on the classic hot dog (Author's Note: Of course, I got a plain hot dog with mustard only. I'll have to go to Cori's a few more times before I venture off the reservation and try something more suited to an adult pallet.).

I sat at one of Cori's colorful tables, pondering life as usual, and all I could think about was how much I admired Sean Sullivan. My hot dog was amazing, and so was his courage. In the same mall in which Cori's is located are at least five other chain restaurants— Red Lobster, Logan's Roadhouse, Olive Garden to name a few— and yet here is a no-name hot dog place bustling with business on a Saturday afternoon.

I asked the woman behind the counter how long Cori's had been in this location. Four years I found out. Four years. That puts Cori's opening in 2009, right after the economic downturn that put a lot of small businesses on the threat of extinction, forget about new start-ups.

I thought about what it might be like to be Sean Sullivan. I don't know his financial background. I don't know his work history, and just in case they ruin the story, I'm not going to find out. But to an outsider it sure looks like Sean Sullivan had a dream to relive his childhood, and he went for it. He started a hot dog restaurant, named it after his daughter, and never looked back.

He has red and yellow furniture, and a big cartoon hot dog running across the walls of his business, and people stand in front of that hot dog and get their picture taken in celebration of their ability to eat forty hot dogs with anything on them from bacon to baked beans.

Think about that for a minute.

Think about what that must have been like at some point in 2008 or 2009 for Sully to tell his wife, "You know what honey, I'm going to open a cross-country themed hot dog restaurant. And I'm going to name it after Cori. We'll have a cool mascot, and I'm even going to buy the red and yellow furniture. People will come from miles around to a suburban mall to eat these gourmet hot dogs."

I don't know about you, but if I were Mr. Sullivan, I would have been expecting to get some pretty wild-eyed looks. And you know what, I'm sure he did. But, four years later, Cori's is still open, and based on the pictures on the Wall of Fame, doing just fine.

Sean Sullivan went for it. In a time when fewer and fewer people actually put their necks out and take risks, Sully took a huge one, and it appears to be paying off.

I grew up at a time when "going for it" really didn't mean much. For nearly my entire life, I knew I was going to go to college. I never really knew what I'd do after college, but I figured I'd do something...

My high school guidance counselors told me what some of the "attractive" career paths were, what other students were pursuing, and which occupations projected to have good long-term viability.

I went to a state university and majored in business. Talk about going out on a limb.

At almost every point in my life, I've asked myself the question, "What's the best decision I can make right now?" Inherently, I'm sure that's not a bad strategy. It's sensible enough. It's definitely "safe" and "logical." I've done alright so far. I have a job that challenges me. I have a career path that has plenty of room for growth. I have a mid-sized sedan and my boss pays for my cell phone. Why should I complain?

In fact, I'm not complaining. I am tremendously thankful for what I have. And, I'm not wishing that I was Sean Sullivan either. I love the life that I have. However, the world needs more Sean Sullivans.

Why is that? Because Sean Sullivan is crazy. Crazy enough to follow his dream. Crazy enough to name his hot dog restaurant after his daughter, and never look back. Crazy enough to buy the red and yellow furniture and plaster a cartoon hot dog running across his wall.

And you know what, Sean Sullivan must be doing something right. Cori's opened their second location just off West End in downtown Nashville.

Way to go, Sully. Keep dreamin' man.

Chewing Gum
in a Strange Concept

There's pretty much no way I was going to get through almost an entire book without at least one entry mentioning Nick Churik. For anyone reading this right now that is not my mother, you have absolutely no idea who I'm talking about. Or, if you went to school with me growing up, you know that a person named Nick Churik exists, but you have absolutely no idea why he's important enough to be mentioned in this book...

Well by now, you probably have figured out that importance and a mention in this book do not have to go hand in hand, but I digress.

Nick Churik represents all that is serendipitous in my life and always will.

Let me explain.

Nick Churik is a kid I was in class with starting in elementary school and ending when we graduated high school together some years later. He lived in the next neighborhood over, his mother and my mother knew each other and he also had a brother who was the same age as my brother. So, as tends to be the case in situations like these, our mothers were friends, so we kind of knew of each other. Nick was a nice enough guy. He hung out with kids that were probably cooler than I was. Unlike me he played football, and we had different groups of friends. I went to a larger high school, and even in middle school there were enough kids and enough classes to the point where you could easily lose track of a kid that you didn't run into on a daily basis.

This is exactly what happened with Nick Churik and me. Last I could remember, we might have played playground football together in third or fourth grade. I can't be too sure. Suffice to say, nothing recent.

My senior year of high school came around, and as my mother is prone to do, she decided to ask a seemingly random question that she deemed to be completely logical: "Have you talked to Nick Churik lately?"

The question caught me off guard. Nick Churik? Why are you asking me about Nick Churik? I haven't talked to Nick Churik since I was in elementary school. "Nooo Mom, I have not talked to Nick Churik. Why would I have talked to Nick Churik? I haven't seen Nick Churik in at least five years. Yeah...I haven't even seen Nick Churik since I got to high school!"

Taken aback by my borderline admonishment, she countered with, "Oh, well, I saw his mother the other day and I just figured I'd ask..."

Okay Mom, I thought. The better part of my judgment decided now was not the time to ask her why she thought her seeing Nick's mother would have anything to with me seeing Nick...These were the types of things I've learned over the years are better left unsaid. Especially to my mother.

Note to anyone who knows my mom: She asks a lot of questions like this. Don't try to answer them. Don't try to reason them out in your mind. In her mind, there is a connection, and while it might not make sense to us, it's not worth getting exasperated over. Dad and Patch, one day you'll learn this...

Anyway, back to Nick. I remember thinking to myself, my gosh, Mom, other than hearing his name on the PA system occasionally being referenced at a football game, that's just not something I had heard in eons.

During our exchange, I could see that my mom was starting to realize that I really didn't want to talk any more about Nick Churik, and she decided to leave things on a motherly note.

"Well, if you see him in the future, tell him I say hi," she said, and that was that.

I visibly rolled my eyes and left the room. Yes, of course Mother, I'll be sure to spot Nick Churik in hallway of high school and call out to him for the first time in more than five years, 'Hey Nick Churik, my mom says to say hi."

Yeah, that would go over well.

The next day. Yes, the very next day, I'm walking down the long hallway at school that connected the counselors' offices to the area where I had my locker. I am alone, and about 20 feet ahead of me in the other direction is a kid wearing a dark sweatshirt.

As I get closer, my jaw starts to drop. It's Nick Churik. For the first time in at least five years, here he is striding towards me. Immediately I became terribly angry. Angry in the sense that my mother does this all the time. She'll tell you it's just because "Mothers know everything," but I think it's something more in this case. I was in my eighth semester of high school at the time, and had somehow managed to never come in contact with Nick Churik, and yet here he was. A day after my mother had mentioned him, he and I were somehow coming face to face, alone in a hallway.

By the time I reached him my anger had turned to laughter. I did one of those "hey" type nods where you kind of say hey as so not to be rude, but you really don't say anything. He did the same, although he looked much more puzzled due to the fact that my "hey" nod came with laughter almost spilling out of my mouth.

He must have been thinking, "What the heck is up with this guy? I haven't seen him in years, and he's laughing hysterically in an empty hallway." Sorry Nick, it wasn't you.

I got home from school that afternoon and angrily began to question my mother. "Guess who I saw today?" I said with much more annoyance than she was accustomed to.

"Who??" she asked, trying to figure out what had me so off kilter.

"NICK CHURIK!" I snarled. "The same Nick Churik I hadn't seen for the better part of a decade! How did you know?"

With a trademark smugness that my mother only shows in situations like these, she kind of tilted her head downward and started to deliver the line that gives her more satisfaction than nearly any other line in the English language. "I'm a mother, and—"

"...mothers know everything!" I cut her off before she could finish. I'd been hearing this idiom since before I was old enough to know what an idiom was.

"Did you say hi for me?" she asked.

At this, I rolled my eyes and walked off. Of course I hadn't said hi for her, but I wasn't going to stick around and be questioned as to why not. To this day, we still joke about Nick Churik whenever something like this happens, and it has become one of our favorite memories as mother and son.

And yes, in case you've been wondering, what does any of this have to do with chewing gum?

Well, this is very similar to the "Family Guy" episode where Peter—in a fashion very similar to my mother—seems to randomly proclaim out loud, "You know what I haven't had in a while?" Before anyone else can answer, he finishes his own question. "Big League Chew!"

I love Big League Chew, and it's probably the only part of "Family Guy" that reminds me of my mother in any shape or form.

The other day, I saw a "Family Guy" clip, and it was the clip of Peter remembering the chewing gum made famous by baseball players. Immediately I thought of how much I loved the gum, and how it had been years since I'd thought of it. Kind of like Nick Churik...

Two days later, I'm at Dick's Sporting Goods checking out at the register, and lo and behold, there's a pouch of Big League Chew. Immediately I'm awe-stricken. How is this possible? I haven't seen this stuff in years?

Is Mom in on this? I haven't been to a Dick's Sporting Goods in months, I never buy the little things that are sold next to the register, and I rarely think of Dick's as a place that sells candy and such. AND I'd just seen the "Family Guy" clip.

How was this happening?

And then I wondered to myself if it had anything to do with the fact that gum chewing itself is just super strange to begin with?

Think about it, maybe gum chewing just brings out the strangeness in all situations.

Gum chewing really doesn't make sense.

Can you think of any other food that you put in your mouth, but don't actually eat?

If you were to do that with any other food, that would be called an eating disorder. Can you imagine an actress going to a restaurant, ordering a steak, and then just chewing it and spitting it out? Tabloids would be all over a story like this. World hunger organizations would protest and within about a week, a promotional company would already be touting the "Chewing Diet."

Not only the whole "not eating" thing makes gum unusual. It's also a toy, a musical instrument, health remedy, a cosmetic aid, a piece of exercise equipment, a very strong adhesive, and a practical joke vehicle that is nearly unrivaled in its own right.

What other foods does society openly allow people to play with while they eat? Any four year old will tell you that playing with your food is a sure sign that you'll end up in time out before the night is up. And yet, you give an adult a juicy wad of chewing gum, and a few minutes later you'll see bubbles start to appear from their mouth as if their four year old swallowed a wand out of a bottle of blowing bubbles.

In a similar vein to blowing bubbles, "gum crackin'" or "popping" can turn into quite the musical spectacle if you assemble the right band. Few things will drive an office full of workers more crazy than an overzealous crowd of gum poppers.

Gum isn't all bad. Manufacturers and their friends in marketing have come up with ways to convince people that chewing gum can medically provide you with fresher breath. On the cosmetic side of things, clinical trials show that in as little as seven days you can actually whiten your teeth by chewing gum. And while I'm not sure if it's ever been marketed this way, chewing gum might be the most effective jaw workout a person can give themselves this side of prom night...

Stick an old piece of gum to the bottom of a chair, and it'll still be there in 40 years. That's better than even the best duct tape...In fact, I'm pretty sure old gum is probably the number one nest building material in most suburban small bird communities. All the best nests have some chewing gum somewhere at their core... (except doves, doves are too lazy for that)

I'm sure there are many other uses for gum that I'm forgetting, but my favorite has to be the bubble gum hat joke. Maybe it's just growing up playing baseball, but there was nothing better than blowing a huge bubble, leaving it inflated, and then stealthily placing it on the head of an unsuspecting teammate. Due to the tremendously low weight of a bubble gum bubble, the victim has no idea something is on their head, and the rest of the team gets to watch gleefully as the bubble sits undiscovered. In today's world, this might be seen as bullying, but for my money, nothing's funnier than a hat bubble.

By these definitions, gum may be the most versatile food in history. I mean, if it's even a food... Immediately after picking up the Big League Chew at the checkout counter at Dick's, I thought of my mom, of the "Family Guy" episode. And then, as if my brain was rewarding me for years of patience during our times apart, I thought to myself, 'I wonder if Nick Churik likes Big League Chew?'

My Perfect Pair of Shoes

I'm not quite sure exactly how it happened, but when I was seven years old, I became obsessed with shoes. Maybe it was Spike Lee as Mars Blackmon, maybe it was watching a lot of Michael Jordan's "Come Fly With Me" VHS highlight tape over and over, but however it happened, my obsession was bordering on absurd by the time I reached second grade.

I'd walk down the street, staring at other kids' shoes and I'd mentally catalog them in my mind. I used to play this game where I'd try to memorize what kinds of shoes all the kids in my school class had. Luckily, second graders don't change shoes that often, so this wasn't that hard of a task.

Somewhere during this time my quest began. The quest for the perfect pair of shoes.

Unlike some people, my shoe obsession did not mean that I

wanted to own many pairs of shoes; it meant that I wanted to own one pair of shoes. The perfect pair. Similar to the way a pimple-covered middle schooler might obsess over the perfect girl, I was this way with shoes. Looking back on this, it's rather odd to me that this developed.

My parents raised my brother, and I very modestly and neither of them immersed themselves in the culture of high style, or material goods. I've come to find out later that my father enjoys fine menswear and especially shoes, but at the time I had no idea about this. My Mom still has some clothes from the Eighties, and while she doesn't wear them in public all that often, I know she takes pride in the fact that clothing and style are more about function than flash. Growing up, our house never had a Glamour magazine, GQ, or anything like that. My dad wasn't big into athletic wear, and until the late Nineties, I'm not sure I ever remember him even having gym shoes. I briefly remember him having a pair of old New Balances in which to mow the lawn, but that was about as close to "athletic" as his shoes got.

So to say that my obsession with shoes was out of left field would be very correct.

I was informed on this topic only by my own observations and in an era before the Internet—and Mom's tight watch over TV consumption—I gleaned most of my shoe knowledge from the other kids at River Woods Elementary School.

Most likely because it's what Michael Jordan wore, I was immediately drawn to Nike. Phil Knight hooked me, and he hooked me good. I had a pair of Nikes when I was maybe five or six, but there was one very significant thing missing: The Swoosh. I'm sure he didn't mean to, but in buying me my first pair of Nikes, my dad had overlooked to coolest detail of the entire shoe: the Swoosh logo.

The Nike logo has evolved over the years. Starting in the early Seventies, the trademark Swoosh appeared on the sides of many running shoes, but for a long time, the logo treatment on the backs of the shoe simply said "NIKE" in a non-descript font.

As the brand has evolved, Nike now often uses the characteristic Swoosh mark on the back of its shoes without any indication that it has anything to do with Nike. It can do this of course because the public already knows what the Swoosh means, so to say Nike would be redundant. Think McDonalds. All you have to see are those golden arches. Spelling out the name is a waste of time.

As a developer of brands, I now understand that this is the ultimate goal—to be so recognizable that you don't even have to say who you are; people already know. Unfortunately for me, I didn't understand this in elementary school.

And unfortunately for my parents, Nike was in a transitional stage as well. Around this time, Nike was pairing their NIKE logo and their Swoosh together on the backs of their shoes. Purposely, I'm not going to provide you with a picture. You know what I mean. The NIKE was surrounded from the bottom up by the Swoosh. You've seen it a million times, I know you have.

Unfortunately on one fateful day in 1992, my parents took me to a shoe store in search of this logo lockup. When we couldn't find it, my obsession turned into something I would battle with for the next 20-plus years. All I cared about was finding the Nike + Swoosh logo.

My dad—unbeknownst to him—found a pair of Air Jordan 7's and asked me if I wanted them. I loved Michael Jordan, and if I would have had any idea about how famous the 7's would have become, I wish I would have had four pairs, but at the time, I passed. They didn't have a Nike + Swoosh. In fact, the entire department store didn't have what I was looking for. I don't remember pouting, but rather I just got frustrated and resigned to the fact that the department store world just wasn't cool enough to satisfy me.

My dad ended up finding a pair of white Nikes with a red tongue with the word Flight printed on it. There was a black Nike Swoosh on the side, but on the back it simply said NIKE. I accepted the fact that these were nice shoes and thanked my dad for buying them for me. Inside, though, I knew something was missing. My dad tried to cheer me up by telling me that these were cool; they said "Flight" on them! But they weren't THAT cool. No shoe without Nike + Swoosh could be that cool.

And so every year or so, the quest for the perfect shoe began.

Five years later, I got my first pair of Air Jordans. The Air Jordan 12. I thought they were the coolest shoes ever made. Even my gym teacher agreed. But they were $90, and that was just a ton of money, and worse yet, they really weren't that comfortable. I loved those shoes, but my heels hurt after wearing them, and they just seemed so heavy!

So then began the quest for a lighter shoe, and I became obsessed with Nike's Zoom Air line. These were designed to be ultralight and ultraresponsive. As a young teenager who was become pudgier by the day, there was nothing about me that said ultralight or ultraresponsive. My basketball career had ended before seventh grade when I was unable to make either of the two levels of the middle school team. Coach Larry Cwik called me into his office after tryouts and informed me that I "Did not have any of the skills necessary to play on the team." I remember telling my friends this, trying to fight back tears, and as middle school kids tend to do, they laughed.

"He actually told you have no skills? Ha-ha. That's awesome," was a common sentiment.

I didn't feel awesome, that's for sure.

So what did I do?

I told my mom I wanted the Nike Zoom Air Turf Jet 97. Yes, this was a turf shoe designed for NFL players to wear on Astroturf in which to play football. No matter that I didn't play football, nor did I play on turf, I wanted this shoe. To complicate things further, my foot had grown to the size of 6-and-a-half. Unaware of this at the time, 6-and-a-half may be the hardest male shoe size in the universe to find.

Kids sizes end at size 6, and most men's shoes technically start at size 7, even those are hard to find. Six-and-a-half is that in-between size for boys who aren't really boys anymore, but aren't really men yet either. This described me perfectly, and my teenage angst came out as I pursued these shoes. My mother, bless her heart, called all over the area asking if anyone had these shoes. This was only after we went to about six stores without any luck. Again, this was the era before online shopping, and my mother was the queen of calling stores asking them to go check their inventory for the item she was after. I can remember she asking a sales person for the Nike Zoom Air Turf Jet and then specifying that it HAD to be in the green color scheme. Again, I didn't realize it at the time, but these shoes would later go down in shoe circles as "The Brett Favres." Hearing my mother asking for them like this would have impressed a young Tony Hsieh, and while Zappos was not yet a business, my mom probably would have earned herself a job there based on her persistence in hunting down these size 6-and-a-half turf shoes for her non-football playing, non-Packer fan teenager who just had to have them.

Finally she found a pair at a store about 30 miles from our house, and being the saint that she was, she drove me out to the store after 8 p.m. to go pick them up.

It was the happiest day of my life.

Except they really weren't comfortable at all. Designed to be lightweight and presumably worn by athletes who wore thick socks, the Turf Jets had virtually no support or cushioning to them at all. They were awful feeling on my feet. But by gosh, we had found them in a size 6-and-a-half, driven almost an hour to get them, and my mom had been on the phone with half of the shoe stores in the state of Illinois just to get this far. I gladly accepted the shoes, and to this day have not uttered a word to anyone as to their discomfort.

The travails of my shoe buying experiences are voluminous, and I will not take you through all of them.

Anyone who has spent any amount of time with me in the last ten years has watched a boyhood obsession turn into an affliction. I very literally almost cannot buy a pair of shoes.

In fall 2004, I was fitted for a pair of Nike Pegasus running shoes. My freshman year of college had gotten me started into serious enough of a running routine to warrant actual running shoes and one of my running friends from college had suggested I get fitted to make sure I got something comfortable.

Man, who knew shoes could feel that good? From that day on, running shoes were really all I could wear on a regular basis. My first pair of Pegasus were terribly ugly, but I didn't care. My feet felt like I was walking on clouds, and for the first time I understood what it meant to have a correctly fitting shoe.

For the last five years I've owned some variation of Nike's Lunar running series. I think Lunar is a play on the moon, and thus the weightlessness that one might feel if they ever walked on the moon. They are great shoes and I've owned various pairs in both grey and orange. Orange became my color of choice in college while attending the University of Illinois, and in an effort to match the rest of my wardrobe, orange shoes only seemed fitting. Even after college, I was drawn to orange simply out of familiarity sake.

But in truth, orange has never been my favorite color. Yellow always has been and always will be.

And in all my years of shoe pursuit, I'd never found a pair of yellow shoes—or even a pair of shoes with yellow as a prominent accent color—to bring my love of shoes and my love of yellow together.

Until yesterday.

As of today as I write this story, I am the proud owner of the most perfect pair of shoes that I have ever owned.

First of all, they are Nikes. They do not have the Nike + Swoosh logo, but in parlance with the times, Nike no longer needs to spell out Nike, so I no longer consider this a criterion for my perfect pair of shoes.

Next, they are built on the familiar Nike Running platform. They are not a part of the Lunar family, but perhaps even better they are constructed on the Nike Air Max framework. Air Max are those large air bubbles that sit in the back of the shoe and cushion your heel. If only my Air Jordan 12s had them! I've never had Air Max before, and it is delightful.

Moving on to appearance, the shoes themselves are royal blue trimmed with a considerable amount of black piping. At a time in my life, blue shoes were an absolute deal breaker, but there's something about this color scheme that I'm in love with.

It gets better. The trademark Swoosh on each side of each shoe is silver inlaid on top of a YELLOW background. Yes, that's right, silver and yellow Swooshes. If Michael Jordan himself came up and handed me a pair of black and red Air Jordan 11's, I don't think I'd be as excited as I am with these Swooshes.

I have spent hours on end in shoes stores looking for this combination. Looking for this perfect mix of function and color and style. My mother has completely given up on mentioning shoe buying in any conversation where it pertains to me. I even wore one pair of old Nikes for five months while they had a hole in the sole because I couldn't decide on my next pair.

But I know these new Nikes are a pair for the ages.

How do I know this?

The shoelaces.

The shoelaces on my new shoes are perfect. They are of perfect length so as not to come untied too easily. Not too long so as to create too large of loops when tying them, and not too short so they won't stay knotted. Each lace is coated at each end with a heavy layer of black eyelet tape. This will keep them protected from moisture for the duration of my ownership experience. And, if it doesn't, the shoes came with a second pair of laces! How lucky could one guy be?

But you know what the best part of the whole deal is? The laces are yellow. Bright, beautiful yellow. Not gold. Not tinted with twinges of brown or orange. Yellow like The Man in the Yellow Hat from Curious George. Yellow like French's mustard. Glorious, glorious yellow.

These laces are the perfect finishing touch to the perfect pair of shoes. It probably doesn't hurt that I got them on sale, or the fact that I saw them, picked them out and bought them in a 10-minute span (Yes, you read that correctly, past, present, and future women in my life, I picked out and purchased a pair of shoes in 10 minutes flat).

All this time, that's what's been missing. The yellow laces make the shoes. I finally solved my riddle. Comfort matters, but above all, it's the laces.

All over the world there are "Sneakerheads" who obsess over noteworthy athletic shoes and there are women who must have the perfect pair of heels. Their pursuits will linger on as fashion designers continue to push the limits of style and beauty. My search for perfection is over, however.

Spike Lee's Mars Blackmon character famously stated in his commercials with Michael Jordan that "It's Gotta be the Shoes!"

No Mars.

It's gotta be the laces.

Embracing the Sweat Stains

I've been thinking for about a week about how I want to end this book. The rest of the book has been written on successive days—the last entry will explain that—but when it came time to write the last story, I needed some time.

I'm not always one who waits before I express my feelings, and in many instances that hasn't always worked in my favor. In the moment, it's easy to say something that isn't necessarily that well thought out.

But at the same time, if I think about things too long I overranalyze them to the nth degree.

So in many ways, this process has been an evolution and a compromise. Writing every day but not publishing or sharing any of it for months. By the time anyone reads these words, it will have been three months since I started writing. While that might not seem like a long time to you—and in terms of publishing a book it's no time at all—to me, that may as well be an eternity.

The biggest thing I've noticed about myself during this process is how much I have grown to love sweat stains.

Yes, you read that correctly. I have really grown to love sweat stains.

Let me explain.

The groundwork for this love was laid when my brother was in middle school track and field. Loosely speaking, he "ran" track, and his event was the hurdles if I remember correctly. I admired my brother for joining the track team. He is three years younger than me, but in many ways has always been an inspiration to me

For a long time, I've had a fear of getting involved in activities. For whatever reason, I have a hard time "just going for it." I think it's probably due to overanalyzing things and being worried about a negative outcome rather than expecting a positive one. I'm working on that now, but back when my brother was in middle school, the thought of my joining a sport or activity I had no previous experience in was as foreign as could possibly be.

I was so proud of him for joining track and I gave him even more credit because he was so, so bad at it. We've laughed about it since then and he excitedly reminds me that he beat a kid once. This wasn't a match race, or a rival, or anything like that. All that means is that one time, in one race, he finished ahead of one kid.

It was after a feat like this that he was able to proudly wear his track team shirt. I love shirts like that. On the front they have the school name and which sport you're associated with and on the back is some team slogan or team saying. We've also laughed in the present day about the fact that this middle school track shirt's slogan was "Pain is temporary. Pride lasts forever!"

The hilarity of these words is never lost on us. Of course, the Madison Junior High track team didn't come up with these words. I'm sure they've been used for generations to inspire world-class athletes to train and compete at the highest level.

The fact that my brother—who is many things, but not a world-class athlete—owned a shirt with this saying on it is just too funny.

As someone whose reluctance to try things kept me from joining many teams, I have always thought these shirts were so cool. More than anything in the world, I wanted a shirt with a cool slogan on it.

I was in high school at the time my brother was running track, and I remember that one of our teams had a shirt that said "Sweat is Pain Leaving the Body."

I don't remember which team it was, and the overly cliché-like nature of the statement ensures that it could have been just about any team. Heck, I'm sure the debate team could have sweat quite a bit outlining some very painful point-counterpoint arguments...

I remember seeing this shirt and wondering how it applied to me. Despite being decently athletic and having been active most of my life, I never really sweat.

I caddied for ten summers in the sweltering Chicago heat, and despite nearly passing out from heat exhaustion on Men's Guest Day in 2000, I barely sweat at all.

To me, sweating was something that old men did.

That day in 2000 when I almost fainted, I was caddying for Tom Garvin. Tom was the former CEO of Keebler, and if the man knew anything better than making cookies and biscuits, it was sweating. Actually, he was a huge fan of track and field as well, come to think of it...

The more I caddied, the more I noticed that old man sweat is super gross. I'll never forget caddying for a man named Will Gillet, who very politely asked me to loop a washcloth around my front left belt loop. I was fourteen at the time and didn't think much of it. I did as I was told and tried not to lose his ball in the tall grass.

About 25 times during that particular round of golf, Mr. Gillet asked me for the wash cloth. He'd wipe his brow, his face and his neck and then he'd hand me back the washcloth to store in my belt loop.

By the end of the round, Mr. Gillet had sweated completely through his golf shirt and his shorts. What started as little dabs of sweat underneath his nipples connected with an ever-expanding circular pool of sweat that started at his belly button. The lower back sweat then made its way around his hips and connected to form a salty suit of armor that may have been able to repel an entire Roman legion.

But it didn't repel me. I faithfully stood by his right hip, and he grabbed for the washcloth on my left hip. Walking down the eighteenth fairway, I started to look to my right to see what time the old clubhouse clock said it was. The clock was rarely right, but I was still too young to know that yet.

I never got to read what time it was because Mr. Gillet needed his sweat rag.

"Hey, Boy!" he said. Old man golfers often referred to their caddies in this way. Trying to remember the name of a hundred caddies is much harder than remembering, "Boy," so I was often just "Boy" or "Sport" or "Pal." This may sound disrespectful, but it rarely was. For his part, Mr. Gillet was one of the kindest men at the club and someone that I would enjoy getting to know over the coming years.

What I did not enjoy was his final request for his washcloth.

"Let me get that rag one more time," he said.

He was a few yards away and up the fairway a bit, but he wasn't walking back toward me. So, to my horror, I had to toss him the washcloth.

Right before you toss a washcloth, you have to grab it a little bit more tightly so that it doesn't fly out of your hand as you swing your arm back to execute the throw. In this case, doing so caused sweat to come pouring out as my strengthened grip wrang the cotton fibers to the point where the cloth could no longer contain all the electrolytes the old man had lost.

I almost puked, but Mr. Gillet was thankful. "Thank you, son" he said. "It sure has been a hot one out here today!"

Yes, yes it had and I was ready for it to be over. What I wasn't ready for was the washcloth, as it came hurling back my way from up the fairway. Mr. Gillet had tossed it back to me and in my state of unawareness, it had landed on my left arm and was slowly sliding towards my left hand. My own saliva curdled in the back of my throat.

I let the rag sort of just settle on my hip and then I picked it up like an investigator might pick up an exhibit of evidence from a crime scene and put it on Mr. Gillet's golf bag. This round was over. I wasn't going to be needing it anymore.

***

So to say I was glad that I wasn't much of a sweater growing up would be an understatement. I'd see people at the gym and out running and they'd be sweating profusely. I never thought much of it. I was thankful I wasn't a sweaty person, but figured it was just good genes or something.

And then it happened.

I started to sweat. A lot. I'm not sure exactly when it started, but it did, and it was a problem.

All of the sudden all my undershirts were heavily stained yellowish brown, even in the neckline area. Really, I thought to myself, my neck is that sweaty that it stains through my shirts?

I haven't changed deodorants. I haven't changed my diet. I haven't gained a lot of weight. But nonetheless, I've turned into a sweaty mess. It's rather off-putting.

It culminated this week.

I've been noticing lately that I've been working out with my T-shirts tucked into my sweatpants. I swore I'd never be that guy, but it's as if all the sudden I'm this middle-aged dork that can't help himself. I never recall tucking my shirt in, but it always seems to happen.

The tucked in shirt keeps the fabric in much tighter than if left untucked, and thus sweat collects in the same concentrated areas.

You can see where this is going.

I now get nipple spots like Mr. Gillet. And belly button pools. And the little trail that connects the two. I came back from a run the other night and I could barely look at myself.

My shirt was dorkily tucked into my pants, which were hiked up unnecessarily high above my hips. The pool of sweat that had formed around my belly button kind of looked like the state of West Virginia, and I could feel a small amount of sweat accumulation up near my collar bones. My hair was actually dripping with sweat, and my glasses were so filthy I probably could have used a pressure washer to get them clean.

The next night, while coaching basketball practice, the same thing happened. I was running with the kids doing a defensive drill and I just started to gush sweat. I looked down at my light blue shirt and saw that it was drenched through.

At first, I was embarrassed. This type of thing happens all the time in gyms, but never to me, so I didn't know what to do.

I felt self-conscious as practice ended, and I quickly hurried to put my jacket on. I walked to my car carrying my basketball and my whistle. The cool air on my moist neck made me uncomfortably cold, but a strange feeling began to come over me.

Two minutes later, I sat in my car. Sobbing. To add to my sweaty mess I was piling tear after tear onto my blue shirt.

These were not painful tears, though. These were tears of joy. I looked down at my sweat-stained shirt. It was gross. I was so gross it was almost intolerable.

Our team colors for the basketball team are light blue and white. As I looked down at the light blue shirt I was wearing, everything came full circle.

All of those teams I'd been afraid to join, all of the pain and uncertainty that I unnecessarily infused into the situations that led to my refusal to try, all of that came pouring out that night.

Not only was I a part of a team, I was a coach of that team. A kid even called me "Coach Troy" that night.

I remembered back to a conversation I had had with my brother a few weeks earlier. He coaches high school soccer, and his kids also call him "Coach Troy."

This thought brought more tears to my eyes. I hadn't told him, but his coaching soccer was what had finally put me over the hump to coaching basketball. My little brother. That same one who could barely clear a hurdle on the middle school track team was that last piece of inspiration I needed to finally conquer a fear that had haunted me for so long.

I looked down at my sweaty light blue shirt. I smiled through my tears and realized what I had just learned.

Sweat IS Pain Leaving the Body.

Writing This Book

I wrote this book for myself, and I also wrote it for you, the person reading it.

For me, I started writing it at a time when I was struggling to see the little things in the big sky. In fact, it felt like there were a lot of little things getting in the way of the big picture. Writing this book helped me realize that the little things are the big picture.

I sat down with one goal in mind when I started writing this book. Every day, I was going to pick something out of my day - no matter how big, how small, or how ridiculous - and write about it. And I was going to try my hardest to make sure that everything I wrote in this book had a positive spin.

There are fifty stories in this book, and I wrote them over the course of fifty-five days. Before work, at lunch, or after work each day, I wrote. I wrote at home, I wrote in parking lots, airports, airplanes, hotels, patios, verandas. No matter what I was doing that day, no matter where I was, I wrote.

I think it probably shows through in the writing too. Some days the stories are humorous, some days they are reflective, some days the stories seemed a little forced, and even others are just flat out ridiculous. Going through this process, I realized, that's a lot like how life is in general. Some days life is funny. Some days it is serious. Other times it tests us, and sometimes there's just no way to explain it.

I tried not to write a negative word in this entire book. And, well, I failed. I rant about a few things along the way, but in general, I think I did alright.

I tried to make each story completely relatable to anyone who might read the book, not just people who know me. I probably failed there, too. I'm sure there are some things in here where people are really going to be scratching their heads!

I tried not to use the same clichés and phrases over and over again, and yet, whatever the case may be... I think I used and yet, and whatever the case may be over, and over and over...

But at the end of the day, despite my flaws, I really enjoyed writing this book. It has helped me re-focus my outlook on the little things in life that make it so great.

I hope that you got something out of it too.

For you, I wrote this book to encourage you to embrace the little things in your life that make you who you are. Chances are, if you wrote this book about your life, you wouldn't go into a long explanation about making up the word 'Nargle' (or narglemuffin for that matter), but I'm sure there are some things deep inside your soul that the world would benefit from learning about you.

It's one thing to share these things with our closest friends, but people often fall short of living as the full version of themselves for the public to see. Obviously there's something to be said for sharing certain parts of who we are with only our closest loved ones, but what about the rest of our lives?

I believe that life is defined by the relationships we cultivate with the people around us. And yes, the people around us includes the mail man, that lady in the deli who has a really big smile, and the guy you see on your way to work every day that always has a different colored pocket square in his suit jacket. Have you ever told him that you love those pocket squares, or asked him where he got them, or maybe told him about the time you used a pocket square as a coaster to try to impress a girl...

The world could use more of these things. There will always be the fight to balance work, life, the checkbook, the datebook, and God forbid trying to find the time to just read a book...

But it's worth it. Sharing the little things is what makes life worth living.

Now put this book down and get to it!

ACKNOWLEDGEMENTS

First of all, I need to thank my editor Rob Bignell for his patience with me as a first-time author. The Craigslist gods were shining down on me the night I found you, Rob and I couldn't have gotten luckier. I appreciate your wit, your wisdom and your commitment to this book! You want to try another one together?

After that, I probably don't have enough room to give everyone else I want to thank an entire paragraph. So I'm going to do it this way:

Barb Scott, thank you for daring me to write in second grade. You encouraged me to be an independent thinker. What do you think, independent enough for you?

John Ballun, thank you for sharing with me a similar book that you wrote. After reading your words, I knew someday I'd find my own.

Chris Blaugh, thank you for urging me to write this summer. Kevin Schaffer, thank you for promising to read this later. This book wouldn't be complete without a BlaughSchaff mention!

Sheri Stewart, thank you for sharing another side of yourself with me. The day after our little chat, I started writing this book.

James Dorn, thank you for giving me the chance to write every day for work. There are probably a few more jokes in here than in our average catalog... This book is electronically formatted because I know if it wasn't, you'd never read it.

Target Check-Out Workers, thank you for assisting me each night as I made my post-writing runs for carrots, crackers and crazy glue. And yes, I do want to save 5% each visit with my RED Card...

Matthew Reilly & David Rosenfelt, thank you for your books that filled my mind with ideas as I was writing my own.

Kati Troy, thank you for your love of childhood memories and family stories. Retelling them together throughout the years has helped me remember so many good times.

Marcy Troy, thank you Mom for never stopping me from asking, why? It's the single most important thing I've ever learned.

Lefty, thank you Pops for your humor, but also for your fatherly advice. This book has so much of your wit and wisdom on its pages and I'm a better man for all of it. Even if Mom won't let you put "Lefty" on your gravestone, at least it's in this book, right?

Jorie Ballun, thank you MJ for encouraging me to look up in the sky and see all the little things.

ABOUT THE AUTHOR

MATT TROY is a zero-time award-winning author. In his free time, he enjoys many of the things written about in this book. Although some things, like ketchup and poorly engineered hotel showers, he does not like. Mr. Troy lives in Nashville. Unlike many authors, he does not have a wife, kids or pets. If and when he has any of those, he'll send you a sticker with their names that you can paste over this paragraph.

www.ingramcontent.com/pod-product-compliance
Lightning Source LLC
Chambersburg PA
CBHW030759150426
42813CB00068B/3251/J